I0464131

NEUROMARKETING ARMOURY

*"Knowledge is a Weapon, John. Arm yourself well
before you ride forth to Battle!"
(op.cit. George, R.R. Martin)*

Dr. HEDDA MARTINA ŠOLA

Dr.Hedda Martina Šola, has asserted her right under the Copyright, Designs and Patents Act 1988 to be identified as the author of this work.

This book is sold subject to the condition that it shall not, by way of trade or otherwise, be lent, re-sold, hired out, or otherwise circulated without the author's prior consent in any form of binding or cover other than that in which it is published and without a similar condition, including this condition being imposed on subsequent purchasers. No part of this book may be reproduced in any form or by any means whatsoever without written permission except in the case of brief quotations embodied in critical articles and reviews. Limitation of Liability/ Warranty Disclaimer: While the author has used her best efforts in preparing this book, she makes no representations or warranties with respect to the accuracy or completeness of the content of this book and specifically disclaims any implied warranties or merchantability or fitness for a particular purpose. The advice and strategies contained herein may not be suitable for your situation. You should consult with a professional where appropriate. The author shall not be liable for any loss of profit or any other damages, including but not limited to special, incidental, consequential, or other damages.

For additional information, please send an e-mail to Dr.Hedda Martina Šola at:

hello@heddamartinasola.com

Copyright © 2017 Dr.Hedda Martina Šola,

All rights reserved.

ISBN-13: 978-1543261899
ISBN-10: 1543261892

The Neuromarketing Science & Business Association (NMSBA) Neuromarketing Publication Series

Brain research, typically appearing under the heading of *neuroscience* or *cognitive science*, has provided us with unprecedented insights into how the human brain works. Neuromarketing brings together and sometimes reinterprets neuroscience findings that are particularly relevant to the field of marketing, creating a new practice.

Neuromarketing touches on all aspects of marketing, from marketing and brand strategy to creative execution, above the line and social media, shopper marketing, package and product design and innovation, and literally anything else a marketer might consider or do. The reason is obvious: all these activities are designed to impact on the consumer's mind – to change the way they feel about the brand, to increase the likelihood of purchase, and even to shape the consumption or usage experience.

It follows that there are many different topics to address when looking at the area of neuromarketing, but all these themes share common ground: understanding and shaping how consumers feel, think and act.

The NMSBA Neuromarketing Series addresses the specialised needs of anyone who leads or supports the marketing effort, including the agencies that often provide essential services in strategy, creative, research and implementation. The Series allows you to select the topics you want to know more about without having to wade through hundreds of pages of material that may be interesting, but ultimately irrelevant to your particular area of responsibility.

We are always interested in constructive comments and suggestions. Please do email us if you have suggestions for future publications, if you are aware of promising new developments, or want to contribute to this Publication Series.

Carla Nagel
Executive Director, NMSBA
carla@nmsba.com

NEUROMARKETING ARMOURY – BOOK REVIEW

When we want to buy a specific product from the shelf on which there are numerous similar products, with all the products having the same use value and all of them having the characteristics which would suit our needs, we opt for one of them without much thinking. Why did we select that very product? What is it that has influenced our decision?

We are exposed to loads of ads every day. However, the fact is that we remember just a few of them, while the majority of them "pass us by" with us not even noticing them. Why is this so? Why did we remember some of the ads, but not the others?

How do we make purchase decisions and why do we purchase specific products?

Such issues have been plaguing both marketing experts and CEOs of the world's largest companies. Finding a way to affect our subconscious desires and being able to influence our purchase decisions would mean solving their major issues.

A new scientific discipline – *neuromarketing* – has been trying to provide us with answers to these issues. Based on contemporary knowledge and scientific achievements in the field of medicine, marketing and technology, neuromarketing has been trying to provide an answer as to the way in which our brain responds to specific stimuli, the part of the brain that responds to, for example, the Mercedes emblem, the Coca Cola logotype or the Snickers chocolate bar wrapper, in what way it does so and what is the intensity of its response.

This book is precisely about such topics from the field of neuromarketing.

The Book *Neuromarketing Armoury,* written by a young author and academic, Dr. Hedda Martina Šola, is the result of years of experience in the field of marketing, and neuromarketing in particular. This is her first book, but what gives it a special value is the fact that this is also the first book on neuromarketing that has been published in Croatia.

Based on specific examples (business case studies), the Author speaks about this topic, providing us with the tools which are used therein and revealing, as she says herself, marketing practice tips and tricks.

For whom this book is intended?

Being written in an original and witty style, but retaining at the same time the required professional and scientific level of expression, as well as taking into consideration the importance and actuality of the topics it covers, this book is a valuable guide for marketing experts and in particular for those who work in the area of neuromarketing because it provides them with specific solutions to some marketing issues or, as the Author likes to say, it: "because it teaches them tricks from the marketing practice".

The Book is intended for professors and students who study marketing as an interesting and useful additional reference. Another proof as to the quality and usefulness of the Book is the fact that you can find it the libraries of most faculties of economics and colleges in Croatia at which marketing is studied.

Owing to the interesting topic and the style of writing used in the Book, we are pleased to recommend the *Neuromarketing Armoury* to a wider reading public wishing to learn the secrets of shopping.

In short, the Book is intended, as the Author says, to all the "smart Alecks" in the area of marketing, as well as to those who are not well-familiar with marketing topics.

Entering the marketing future through which we are skilfully and confidently guided by the Author, let's enjoy the reading of this Book because when we start reading we will not be able to stop. I have read it in one sitting with great pleasure, driven by my professional curiosity. I truly believe that you will do the same.

Therefore, let the Author skilfully guide you through the labyrinth of secrets and interesting facts about neuromarketing.

After you have read the Book, you will inevitably raise the following question: "Is there an end to the traditional marketing in sight?" According to the suggestions made by the Author of this Book, the answer to this question is a positive one.

Therefore, we can say the following:

Goodbye, the traditional marketing!

Hello, neuromarketing!

Knowing the Author's will and perseverance, as well as her professional and scientific potential, I am convinced that we will not be waiting too long for us to be presented by the Author with her next (equally interesting) book because there is much more she can tell us about neuromarketing.

Doc.Dr. Ivan Matković
The Book Editor
Docent at the Hercegovina University,
Faculty of Social Sciences, Mostar.

DEDICATION

I dedicate this book to my son Gabriel and my husband Ilija who have supported me throughout the entire process of writing this book (each in his own way! J). I also dedicate it to my aunt, Miroslava Zajec, M.D. in ophthalmology,who has always been my role model and my other mother. I dedicate it to my dearest ones who are not amongst us anymore, but who keep living in my heart: to my late mother, Prof. Jasna Klemsa, M.Sc. and to my late grandmother, Prof. Đurđa Sertić.

CONTENTS

ACKNOWLEDGMENTS

I must admit that for me this is the most important part of my book because without all these people my book would not be what it is. I wish to acknowledge my indebtedness to the world-renowned academic and professional experts in neuromarketing who have enriched my book with their valuable reviews and have given their final contribution to it. I am very proud that my book has been reviewed by these very reviewers, and I am deeply grateful to them for finding the time for my book amid their numerous professional, academic and other commitments, as well as their commitments as authors themselves! My sincerest thanks are due to Dr. Peter Steidl who has been a great support to me throughout the entire process of the writing of my book, and without whose efforts, affability and understanding for all my questions, my book would not have been published so soon. I am also grateful to Prof. Dr. Benny Breisemeister who has impressed me very much with his propriety and his willingness to be my reviewer! Moreover, despite his busy schedule, he has found the time for my book and has even given it priority! Grateful thanks are expressed to Prof.dr.sc. Ivan Matković who has kindly assisted me in the editing of my book in addition to writing a review, which has not been an easy task!

I would like to express my gratitude to Mrs. Carla Nagel, Executive Director at Neuromarketing Science and Business Administration, who has recognised the value of my book and has included it into the NMSBA Publication Series. I would also like to thank Prof. eng. ita. Željana Šurlan, Ec. S. who has succeeded in transmitting my spirit when translating the book from Croatian into English. I also wish to thank Mrs. Smiljka Božičković who has managed to communicate the title of my book owing to her creative book cover design.

Dr. Hedda Martina Šola
February, 2017.

FOREWORD

The book you are holding represents an amalgamation of my twenty-year experience in marketing, as well as many years of scientific research in neuromarketing. This book contains a summary of the best professional and scientific papers I have published, as well as my papers which are getting published for the first time. This book is not intended to be read in one sitting, since it will certainly leave you breathless, but as a manual you will use in day-to-day business, reading the chapters you find essential for your business activity. The book also contains numerous tests which may help boost your brain's creativity in solving marketing problems (determining the retail price, market positioning, product design etc.), as well as a number of techniques assistant professors can utilise in their exercises at the faculty. The Croatian edition of this book was published under the title *Marketinška oružarnica*. The book *Neuromarketing Armoury* is a redesigned version of the Croatian original.

This book will teach all of you who have been in business for a long time now the marketing practice tricks!

To all of you who are studying, it will serve as additional bibliography worth reading and aimed at training you in marketing!

And you, dear readers, who are just like me, and want to know what science and professional practice have been both revealing and hiding – THIS BOOK IS FOR YOU!

FASTEN YOUR SEAT BELTS! WE ARE ABOUT TO TAKE OFF! J

INTRODUCTION

In 2002, the Daimler Chrysler Research Center wanted to explore further in detail the brain of the consumers who buy their cars. They conducted a research in which they showed the pictures of sixty six different sports cars to men of about the same age, and scanned their brain using the Functional Magnetic Resonance Imaging (fMRI) procedure. However, they discovered something really amazing! Something which has changed....EVERYTHING! Among all the luxury cars (Ferrari being one of them), Mini Cooper has won! How did they do it?? The results of the analysis have shown that all the participants in the survey who underwent the fMRI procedure having seen the picture of a Mini Cooper, showed a relaxed facial expression.

Further research has shown that instead of a Mini Cooper, what the respondents actually see is a "small glowing creature", a "four-wheel Bambi", or "Pikachu with an exhaust pipe!"

[1]In marketing, it has been proven a long time ago that children's faces have got a strong impact on our brain. However, a Mini equals a four-wheel Bambi?? Yes, indeed! Let's move on.

The same research has shown that the reason why customers buy sports cars is that they stimulate a part of the brain which can be described best using the expression such as "a reward and reinforcement"[2]. In behavioural psychology, the reinforcement is the consequence that will reinforce the future behaviour of an

19

organism in case a specific behaviour was preceded by a certain stimulus or trigger. As you can see, brands represent far more than mere product design and packaging. In order for us to be able to compile a "cook book" which may provide answers to questions such as: "why do some brands achieve success, while others fail?", it would be helpful if we had a better understanding of what was really going on in our brain when deciding whether we would buy something or not. Take a look at the following example: you are lying on the couch, watching a film. You feel warm and comfortable. Your appetite is fully satisfied.

Suddenly, a sad scene appears on TV (in the film you are watching). You start crying. WHY? WHY ARE YOU CRYING?! Most of you will reply something like: "I got emotional".

Marketing experts (marketers) will say the following: "they have used emotional appeals in order to obtain response from a consumer." Hm...do you know what I would say? I would say that you have just been hypnotised without even being aware of it! Yes, you have! There are TV commercials and films which have got a hypnotic effect onto the consumers with the purpose of achieving a "better positioning" of their brand (product brand) in our brain. There are products and TV commercials the consumers cannot keep their eyes off. There are commercials the consumers watch almost without blinking. For this very purpose the *Neuromarketing Armoury* was written!

As we can learn from the study of history, since the beginning of time, wars have been waged in a very simple way: the war's outcome between the two warring sides depended exclusively on their number. If we compare it to marketing, we can say that in the past the so-called "advanced" techniques used in marketing were sufficient enough (it was essential to have as large advertising campaign as possible, as many products as possible etc.). Today, it is not crucial to be the greatest, the most numerous, but to possess new "weapon" (new knowledge)!

The time has finally come in which even the small businesses, not only the large ones, have started utilising the valuable knowledge from the area of neuromarketing (brain testing, brain stimulation). This book has been designed "as an armoury" for your new weapon (new knowledge) which you will utilise regardless of your marketing requirements. Regardless of whether your goal is to bring your product closer to the customer or to position your company on the market, this book represents the essence of my scientific and professional research with the purpose of elaborating specific details which are indispensable in marketing.

It is not important to be big and strong anymore! With the new "weapons" and new rules of "warfare" being available, your strength lies in your very knowledge!

Therefore, welcome to the Neuromarketing Armoury! The selection is wide, customers are numerous, the time is running out, but your gain is priceless!!!

CHAPTER 1

MONKEYS IN A CAGE

Key topics covered by this chapter

- ✓ An experiment with five monkeys and a banana
- ✓ How a monkey improved marketing
- ✓ New age advertising: IGA!
- ✓ G.I.A. – The Girls Intelligence Agency ?!
- ✓ Hide-and-Seek!

MONKEYS IN A CAGE

*It is not enough to have a good mind; the
main thing is to use it well.*

Imagine a cage in which five monkeys are placed. In the middle of the cage, a banana is hanging on a rope, while a ladder is placed beneath the banana. The only way the monkeys can reach the banana is by climbing the ladder. Before long, one of the monkeys starts climbing the ladder in order to reach the banana. However, as soon as the monkey approaches the ladder (trying to reach the banana), the scientists spray all the monkeys with a jet of cold water! Soon, though, another monkey attempts to get the banana. As soon as he touched the ladder, once more the scientists sprayed all the monkeys with cold water again! Afterwards, whenever one of the monkeys attempted to reach the banana, the others tried to prevent him. What you need to do is remove one of the monkeys from the cage and replace him with a new one. As soon as the newcomer spots the banana, he will try to grab it. Much to his surprise, the other monkeys will attack him. The newcomer will try to grab the banana a few more times, but when he realises that he will get beaten up, the monkey will give up.

The next thing you need to do is replace yet another monkey with a new one. The new monkey will also try to reach the banana, but the others will attack him, as usual. Even the monkey that was penultimate to enter the cage and did so enthusiastically, was punished eventually! So now we are going to replace all the original monkeys with new ones. Each newly arrived monkey that gets close to the ladder will be attacked! The other monkeys that attack him haven't got the slightest idea why it is forbidden to climb the ladder, or why they participate in punishing each newcomer who makes an attempt to do so (since not one of the monkeys among the ones that replaced the original ones was ever sprayed with cold water).

Nevertheless, none of the monkeys is trying to get the banana! Why is that so? It is so because the monkeys in the cage have always been governed by these rules![3] Therefore, what is it that prevails in your case? Is it marketing, or monkeys?!

This represents one of the striking examples of marketing and monkeys which shows that in most business organisations there are some common rules (now you can decide for yourself whether they refer to marketing or the monkeys :-)), by which organisations have been governed nowadays, although most employees find it difficult to understand them, or they question their appropriateness. Marketing has taught us that knowledge that a specific company has acquired becomes a crucial factor in business. It is this knowledge that makes a company unique in the market and distinguishes it from all the other companies.

If we call to mind the following slogan: "Every day, if not every hour, in almost all the organisations, information is under the influence of power, politics, and economics. This is not a secret"[4], the question arises, which is as follows:

Do we really know what is the information we need, the one which is relevant, and how to obtain it?

HOW A MONKEY IMPROVED MARKETING?

200 years ago, Jean-Baptiste Say, a French economist and a successful businessman (1767-1832) coined the term "entrepreneur", denoting a person who introduces agitation and disorganisation into business. Later on, Joseph Schumpeter, an Austrian-born American economist and political scientist declared this procedure a "creative destruction"[5]. In other words, in order for you to be able to achieve something new, you need to eliminate all which is old, worn-out, unproductive, along with the old habits, errors, and the paths which had led you astray.

Unfortunately, cold water is still being sprayed onto managers with fresh ideas, or anyone else who tries to introduce something new. Such behaviour makes employees keep their ideas to themselves, and the company cannot survive on the market in the long run.

Do you know what are the two ways in which you can sabotage any project?

1. Assign the wrong role (to any individual) and prevent him or her from accessing all the relevant sources of information;
2. assign the right role (to any individual) and overload him or her with a wealth of useless information.

Eventually, the effect will be the same. It is precisely for this reason that it has become important and extremely necessary to establish a system of business information management in marketing (business intelligence). Now, in order for you to make sure that you have mastered the most important principles and techniques of introducing marketing and monkeys to your business organisation, test yourself by answering the following question:

What do I know about the XY company?

Wrong answer: The task has already been defined. (So we can begin the process of gathering all the relevant data on specific competitors.)

Correct answer: What kind of business decision do we intend to make, or what seems to be the specific business problem? (Only then can research be conducted according to specific requirements.)

NEW AGE ADVERTISING: IGA (IN-GAME-ADVERTISING)!

Consumers are conditioned during their first year of development... Children begin their first journey as consumers in early childhood. And they certainly deserve to be considered consumers from this very moment.

(- James U. Mcneal, a Youth Marketing Pioneer)

There are products and TV commercials children cannot look away from. There are TV commercials which reduce the blink rate in children while watching them. There is also a kind of products which children indicate as a "must have", knowing they will obtain them if they repeat their requests persistently. All of the afore-said happens for a reason. For example, neuromarketing researchers use a blink count technique which measures the blink rate in children while watching a specific TV commercial. If the blink rate is high, they adapt the TV commercial with the purpose of achieving a better hypnotic effect.

On the other hand, psychologists, anthropologists, sociologists and child behaviour scientists, along with marketing and advertising experts, have been working together in order to spur children's interest in particular brands in the easiest, fastest, and most direct way. They all want to occupy a so-called "part of the mind" in a child, particularly as marketing experts have proved that children can recognise names as they turn 6 months old.

The marketing profession utilises cutting-edge testing equipment for the purpose of testing and monitoring children in order to be able to identify a specific structure of shapes, colours, music, words, and alliteration which the children cannot resist (op. cit. "Consuming Kids –the Commercialization of Childhood"). Commercials belong in the past – they are typical of the 20th century.

In-game Advertising (a combination of games and advertisements), symbols used in advertising, the G.I.A. and the introduction of products into a television or a video programme, are all part of the new age advertising. According to the statistics published in the USA, we can conclude that today there are more than 52 million children (aged under 12) who spend approx. 40 billion USD on purchasing goods and services. Research has also shown that the spending by adults whose purchasing decisions are directly influenced by children under 12 has increased significantly, with an annual spending rate of 700 billion USD in total. If we do a little bit of maths and do a comparative economic analysis of the GDP (Gross Domestic Product) of a product (a macro-economic measure of the total value of goods produced or services provided within a specific time period, usually a year) for each country, the total expenditure amounting to 700 billion USD bears a striking resemblance to the cumulative sum of the 115 poorest countries in the world. Accordingly, we can conclude that children are the consumers of tomorrow!

They are future adult consumers of a given company's products and services. In 1970, the advertising of products to children was very limited. Today, however, in advertising, much attention is given to each age group separately. For example, there is a big difference in advertising a particular product to a three-year-old and to a five-year-old child: the commercial aimed at a three-year-old must be presented at a slower frame rate than the one addressing a five-year-old, and it must be designed using round shapes instead of the sharp ones etc. At this age, children absorb all kind of information like "little sponges" and manufacturers are striving to gain their loyalty towards a given brand for a lifetime. For this very reason, much attention is given to marketing to children.

Let's take a look at several different media through which the advertising campaign may convey its message to children. They are as follows:

1. presenting of an advertising campaign in films,

2. presenting of an advertising campaign in video games,

3. advertising at nurseries and in schools,

4. licensed brands,

5. viral marketing (in other words, the campaign advertising a specific product spreads like a virus),

6. i-Pod.

Today it is much easier than before to broadcast an advertising campaign through media channels because today children use several different media at the same time; for example, while being on the Internet, they watch TV, listen to music on an iPod, exchange text messages on their mobile phones as they consume a brand licensed product.[6]

G.I.A. – "THE GIRLS INTELLIGENCE AGENCY" ??!

Having its registered Head Office in Los Angeles, to this date the G. I. A. has had 40,000 registered members, the so-called "secret agents" across America aged 8 to 29. It was founded with the purpose of helping hundreds of large corporations strategically reach their customers. The companies such as Nestlé, Procter & Gamble, Mattel, Lego, Sara Lee, Johnson & Johnson, Dreamworks, Disney, Warner Brothers, Sony etc., are just a few among many whom the G. I. A. has helped reach their sales and marketing goals. You must be wondering how the G. I. A. operates.

With an annual cost amounting to 159 billion USD, the G. I. A. has been cooperating with the girls whom they ask to test a certain product or to form product testing groups just for fun in which they invite children to give their opinion on a specific product. They gather data on a specific product from their friends working as "secret agents", without their friends knowing what they do. As a reward, they obtain money or free products (Juliet Schop, Ph.D., Prof. of sociology, Boston College).[7]

– HIDE-AND-SEEK – THE ADVERTISING OF TOMORROW

If we consider the role, subject and goal of advertising in marketing to children in the past, we can conclude that companies have moved significantly beyond the type of advertising which uses exaggeration to emphasise a product's features, and now a completely new chapter has opened up using a brand new form of advertising. The familiar mantra in marketing is the following: "You are what you've got. You are what you buy. You are what you own." (Velma Point, Ph.D., Prof. Of Education, Howard University).

The American Psychological Association (APA) has stated that showing TV commercials to children under the age of 8 should be banned, since it has been proven that at that specific age children are incapable of understanding that the marketer wants to sell them a specific product, and they perceive the TV commercial as real. The results of numerous studies have indicated that children aged two to three start watching TV more frequently, spending an average of 2.5 to 3.0 hours a day in front of the screen.[8]

"Children are actually influenced by their peers and the wider community, while family communication – which is predominantly non-dialogic in nature – is mainly focused on everyday issues and matters of perspective (Ilišin, 2003: 30), so we return to the beginning of the story which shows that the impact of TV commercials on the social, emotional, as well as the cognitive development of children and adolescents is too forceful."[9]

"An analysis of Croatian TV commercials targeting children and adolescents has shown that they often utilise popular children's TV characters to transfer the illusion of reality presented in cartoons and films for children into the real world and onto a specific product, distinguishing it from a multitude of other products in the same category (which may be of better quality and/or more affordable). Often, the contents of the product itself becomes less important if the packaging shows superheroes who are popular with children. Modern means of communication and technology are more advanced than ever before.

Still, TV commercials often offer a world which differs significantly from the one where the children live with their family. The world which is presented to them is much more fun and more dynamic, and it is a kind of world in which the child is placed at the centre of events:[10]

- Conjure up some crazy and spooky fun with Bratzillaz dolls. These enchanting witches will cook up a magic fashion and show you the world where glam gets wicked!
- It is time for a crazy millennium party!
- It is Draculaura's birthday, and your favourite characters are getting ready for an unforgettable party! Are you ready to test your ingenuity against your opponents?"

CHAPTER 2

NEUROMARKETING

Key topics covered by this chapter

✓ Welcome to the world of Neuromarketing!

✓ We can blame it all on the Amygdala?!

✓ How about a pack of cigarettes with a picture of the lungs?

✓ Hurray! Neuromarketing & practice

✓ Scientific research in Neuromarketing

✓ What can PR Learn from Neuromarketing?

NEUROMARKETING

WELCOME TO THE WORLD OF NEUROMARKETING!

If you wish your customers to make the right decision and buy your own product, provide them with the right reasons!

Have you ever felt uncomfortable because advertisers knew exactly how to arouse a sense of purchase in you through their advertisements (although you were not even planning to buy that specific product or service)? Have you ever had that familiar feeling of being so fascinated by a specific TV commercial that you had to go immediately to the store and search for THAT VERY product? Just wait: IT'S JUST THE BEGINNING!

The Russian psychologist Ivan Pavlov, after whom "Pavlov's theory" was named, demonstrated the producing of a conditioned response on the example of dogs, which has showed that if we transfer the analogous situation onto humans, we can conclude that, for example, the scent of a dinner being cooked will make your mouth water, or if you are eating dinner while watching the news, you could eventually start associating dinner with the news. Most of you are familiar with the fact that using the so-called "rational appeal" in TV commercials is sometimes more efficient than using the so-called "emotional appeal". Of course, it all depends on the type of the target audience you are addressing, as well as their level of interest in a specific type of product. The marketing profession and science have proved that reasonable appeals are more efficient in educated audience, while emotional appeals (such as fear, sense of humour, aggressive advertising, sex in advertising etc.) achieve greater success among a less educated target audience.

However, science and the marketing profession have taken a major step forward and have gone one step further. After years of research on the way in which the consumers make unconscious purchasing decisions, marketing, as a profession and as a scientific discipline, has managed to crown its work by introducing the neuromarketing discipline: together with neuroscientists and clinical psychologists.

Neuromarketing is a discipline which has spread across Europe, and which utilises human brain *scans* for the purpose of measuring the impact of a specific TV commercial on the consumer. On the other hand, to the companies that wish to increase their sales, neuromarketing offers the possibility to perform a quantitative assessment of consumers' attitudes, as well as the efficiency of commercials and advertising campaigns even before you start making plans to spend large sums of money on leasing ad space (which has been common practice so far).

This has been a great help to marketing experts who always worry about whether the results of the assessment (they had entrusted to a market research agency) of their campaigns are really relevant or not. Branding expert and NY Times best - selling author Martin Lindstrom, has proven scientifically that 90% of consumers make their final purchase decisions at an unconscious level.

More precisely, from the moment we enter a store till the moment we reach the final purchase decision, it takes less than 4 seconds, which means that there is no way in which we can explain whether our purchase decision was made by acting rationally or not. All the decisions we make are the result of the activity of the primitive part of the brain which is responsible for unconscious thinking.

Now you will exclaim, "THE PRIMITIVE PART OF THE BRAIN??!" Exactly! One of the most important senses which we use when making decisions – for example, we may or may not trust people or situations – is our very visual channel. The optic nerve contains a million nerve fibers in comparison to the auditory nerve which contains only 30,000 nerve fibers. The visual processing speed at which our brain receives and decodes a certain piece of information is measured in milliseconds (ms).

For the time period under 300 ms, we cannot understand the process, or at least a large part of what we have seen using our advanced cognitive functions.

This is where the critical aspect lies, in the way in which we use visual processing functions in decision-making.[11]

WE CAN BLAME IT ALL ON THE AMYGDALA?!

Within a study conducted by Princeton University12, a survey was carried out about the way in which we decode the faces we trust with respect to the ones which evoke negative connotations in us, and it has been observed that as part of this process there is an organ which is found in the most primitive part of our brain (it is called amygdala), that decides who is a positive person, and who is a negative one based on something which is known to us or which evokes a pleasant sensation in us.

You read right! The organ which is found in our most primitive part of the brain! The research study conducted has shown that the amygdala was activated only 100 ms after the pictures had been shown to test subjects. Significant findings obtained in the study have shown that most of the decisions we make and we stick to are triggered by our very visual senses, and without the involvement of our centre of consciousness.

This may explain why we are in such a state that, when we see a picture in the newspapers, we are able to write a news article about it, without having read the news itself. Now, once you know that the most primitive part of our brain is the one which makes final decisions, your marketing and sales strategy can assume completely different principles of communication in order to be impressive.

Figure 1: a computer-generated picture of the faces we perceive as (un)trustworthy

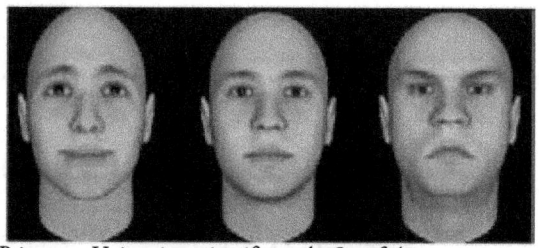

Source: Princeton University, scientific study. See cfr4.

The study has proven that, when shown the observed sample, most of the participants in the study opted for the person in the picture on the far left as the one they perceive as the most trustworthy, perceiving the picture in the middle as neutral, and the person in the picture on the far right as the least trustworthy.

Table 1. Methods in neromarketing

TYPE OF METHOD	SUBCATEGORY	EXPLANATION
Biological fMRI	EEG – electroencephalography	Though brain imaging we have obtained data on a spontaneous electrical activity during a brief period of time upon making a purchase decision.
	MEG (magnetoencephalography)	Measures the magnetic fields which produce electrical activity of the brain upon making a purchase decision.
ECONOMIC	GAME THEORY	Simulated situations for detecting the behaviour of individuals in which success depends exclusively on the selection of someone else.
PSYCHOLOGICAL	Various studies on behaviour and analyses	

Source: Šola, H.M., 2013. Neuromarketing – science and practice.
FIP – Scientific Journal of Effectus College for Law and Finance with international peer-review: Volume 1, ISSN 1849-241 X.

There are three broad categories which enable the procedure of consumer testing in neuromarketing:

1. Localisation – it studies the part of the brain which is necessary for provoking a behavioural response
2. Association–it studies the interaction of different parts of the brain which use an established pattern in information processing

3. Presentation –it studies information which is stored in the brain, and which represents the so-called "codes" that drive the information.

It is worth mentioning that understanding these very "codes" is crucial for several neuroscientific achievements, especially in "interpreting" current thoughts and experiences of individuals, in order to be able to assess their mental state at the moment of stimulation of an experimental subject (by commercials and products) in real time.[13] Neuroscientists have demonstrated that there are three parts of our brain which are interrelated, and each of them performs a specific function.

"The new brain" thinks. From the moment it receives information, it processes only rational data, sharing the data filtered in such a way with the other two brains.

"The middle brain" feels. It processes emotions and only the positive feelings which it shares with the other two brains.

"The old brain" decides! It takes suggestions from both brains (the middle one and the new one), but it is the only one controlling the decision-making process.

Once you get to know that "the old brain" is the one that makes the final decision, the marketing and sales strategy may take on completely different principles of communication, in order for them to be impressive.[14]

Marketing analysts will be using neuromarketing with the purpose of obtaining more precise measurements of consumer' preferences instead of a verbal reply to the following question: "Do you like this product?" Due to cognitive bias, in most cases, this question does not necessarily produce honest answers. Such information may be very helpful to marketing experts in designing products and services, in order for them to create far more efficient ones, as well as to place a special emphasis onto brain's response in promotional campaigns.

Neuromarketing will provide answers to the following questions: "How do consumers respond to your product, to its colour, design or packaging, to the sound or the idea, that is, what is it that the consumers prefer you had got, but you haven't?" We live in a world in which companies more o less routinely announce their commitment to buyers. However, we also live in times in which the buyers' expectations are not sufficient anymore for us to be able to win their loyalty (attachment) to a specific brand or product.

This is what makes us commit ourselves to greater sincerity, authenticity and total engagement. Still though, some experts believe that the knowledge of a mechanical part of the consumer's brain is sufficient enough, enabling them to get the client to do precisely what they have in mind. Unfortunately, most large businesses consider neuromarketing a new chapter in the old-trick practice, where the client is seen exclusively as an object the tradesmen believe they can do whatever they like with. Neuromarketing is a discipline which is to be treated as an addition to marketing research, and as such, it should produce the most realistic results and avoid violating the code of ethics, since it would not be based exclusively on manipulation, but would use such data in a way to manufacture and sell the products preferred by shoppers. Instead of dealing exclusively with the brain of their buyers, marketing experts should rather focus on their hearts: in order for them to develop a financially justified product the buyer considers to be worth waiting for in a queue in order to be able to buy it.

Buyers are far more intelligent and rich than ever before. You need to pay them the same respect you would to a partner in a reciprocal relationship. You need to regard them as individuals, not as machines, appealing to their competence in decision making. [15]

Therefore, if you wish your potential buyers to make the right decision and buy your own product, provide them with the right reasons!

HOW ABOUT A PACK OF CIGARETTES WITH A PICTURE OF THE LUNGS?

For many years now, the pictures appearing on cigarette packs have been used for the purpose of raising awareness in smokers of the harmful effects of smoking on people's health. "Smoking causes lung cancer","Smoking causes blindness and impotence", "Smoking during pregnancy causes birth defects in children." These are all just "gentle" warnings, unlike most of the labels on cigarette packs in Canada, Thailand, Brasil and Great Britain. In those countries, cigarette packs carry original colour graphics showing foot gangrene, lung cancer or open wounds with tooth decay being the consequence of throat cancer. In 2006, tobacco companies worldwide, together with the governments of several countries, invested millions of euros in smoking awareness campaigns.

Approximately 15 billion cigarettes are sold per day, which, in mathematical terms, means that 10 million cigarettes are sold every minute! In China, as many as 300 million people still believe that smoking cures various diseases (such as Parkinson's disease, it mitigates the symptoms of schizophrenia etc.), and with annual sales of 1.8 trillion cigarettes, China's tobacco monopoly is responsible for 1/3 of all the cigarettes sold around the world. It does not make any sense at all! Are the smokers blind, and therefore not able to see all those campaigns and warnings written on the pictures which appear on cigarette packs, or do they think they are immortal?! Or is it perhaps the fault of neuromarketing? The largest study ever conducted in neuromarketing was based precisely on the study of this issue. In the time period from 2004 to 2007, 2081 volunteers (smokers), supervised by dr. Gemma Calvert from the University of Warwick (England),who is also professor of neuroscience at Oxford, with a total budget amounting to 7 million USD (donated by 8 multinational companies), together with top marketing experts, made an amazing discovery![16]

Do you believe that covert advertising (*product placement*) of products in TV shows is producing excellent results in sales? The answer is "no"! Do you believe that brand logos have got strong influence on consumers? You will be shocked: not anymore! Smell and sound have got much stronger influence on consumers!

Does subliminal advertising wield influence on them? Yes, it does, but it wields the greatest influence on the shopping you did the previous day. You didn't know this, did you? Does sex still have great power in advertising? Not really. Then what should be done in advertising in order to encourage shoppers to buy products? Let's get back to cigarettes, as this is where the formula is! Participants in the study were subjected to two types of tests: the ones using questionnaires (a common pattern of behaviour in marketing) and the ones using fMRI (functional magnetic resonance imaging). Why is this important? The marketing profession has shown that questionnaire respondents provide subjective feedback which depends on their mood, not on their actual opinion.[17]

This is very important because if you take a look back at what you have learnt about marketing, such as the fact that buyers make decisions at an unconscious level, you will discover that it is important to take a peek into the consumers' brain. And that's where fMRI comes in, measuring the quantity of oxygen in the brain of all the participants who were shown various labels found on cigarette packs from all angles. Well???? What are the results? The analysis has shown that warning labels on cigarette packs had no influence whatsoever on smokers! Nothing! So, none of the graphic images, studies, labels, government measures, have any influence whatsoever on smokers! However, now you are wondering where is the formula? Read on. The analysis has not proven this information alone, it has proven that (brace yourselves for the shocking news which you are about to receive) the labels appearing on cigarette packs with warnings which highlight the dangers of smoking, including lung cancer, death etc. actually stimulate a part of the brain, called the *nucleus accumbens*, also known as the region which generates desire. This region of the brain is located in the vicinity of all the neurons which get activated when the body is moved by a desire: such as alcohol, a cigarette, sex etc. When it is activated, the nucleus accumbens requires ever as larger doses in order to be able to calm down! So, the results of the analysis of fMRI have shown that labels on cigarette packs do not reduce smoking rates at all, but, on the contrary, they activate the region of the brain which increases a desire for a cigarette! The same study has also shown that the respondents, when answering the questions in the survey, answered affirmatively to the questions about the pictures, claiming they were gruesome, and that they reduced smoking because of them, while the results of brain scans showed quite the opposite.

Does this mean that respondents lied?

No, it only proves that, on a conscious level, our brain is saying what it thinks it knows, while the formula is actually in the unconscious part of our brain, since it knows and decides.[18]

HURRAY! NEUROMARKETING & PRACTICE

After years of research on the way in which consumers unconsciously make purchase decisions, marketing as a profession and a scientific discipline has managed to crown its work by introducing a new discipline of economics: neuromarketing.

The term "neuromarketing" was devised by Ale Smidts In 2002. It's neuromarketing NY Times best selling author is Martin Lindstrom. His three-year study costed Oxford University more than 7 million dollars, which were donated by eight multinational companies. Lindstrom has used the cutting-edge technology of modern day medicine, and he scanned more than 2,000 experimental brains which were subjected to various marketing strategies which included the following: product positioning, the influence of subliminal messages, non-original brands and logos, health and safety warnings, a provocative design and product packaging.[19]

Lindstrom has integrated the results of research into his new book[20] in which he has proven that 90% of consumers make their final purchase decisions solely on the non-conscious level. We can conclude that, from the moment we enter a store to the moment we make the final purchase decision, it takes less than 4 seconds (s), meaning that there is no way in which one could rationally explain that we are capable of thinking about the purchase in a rational way. All the decisions which we make are proven to be the result of the primitive part of the brain with no centre of consciousness.

Consequently, we can conclude that neuromarketing initiates where traditional marketing techniques of consumer research expire. Neuromarketing initiates in the brain and perception of consumers.[21]

THE IMPACT OF NEUROMARKETING ON THE PROMOTION OF A MARKETING CAMPAIGN

The marketing profession has proven that neuromarketing techniques have a direct impact on the following: product development, graphic design, product distribution and promotion in general. If marketing promotion is performed through billboards, the techniques used in neuromarketing science depend on the location and duration of the campaign. Neuromarketing methods and techniques have a different effect on each type of marketing promotion, as elaborated in detail below:

Table 2. The impact of neuromarketing on promotion

TYPE OF PROMOTION	IMPACT OF NEUROMARKETING
Promotion through TV/radio ads	• Radio station selection • Ad length.
Promotion through Internet	• Ad content • Promotion length.
Point-of-sale promotion	• Selection of the location for product promotion • Product selection.
Sponsorship	• Selection of a celebrity • Popular events.

Source: Reynolds, J., 2006. Measurement and Analysis for Marketing. Journal of Targeting, Vol. 14 No. 3, pp. 189-90

Table 3. The impact of neuromarketing on graphic design

TYPE OF PROMOTION	IMPACT OF NEUROMARKETING
Promotion through billboards	• Billboard size • Colour distribution • Marketing message • Selection of a celebrity.
TV commercial promotion	• Message length • Product selection-focus • Information/entertainment ratio • Colour distribution • Pictures • TV presenter/music.

Source: Reynolds, J., 2006. Measurement and Analysis for Marketing. Journal of Targeting, Vol. 14 No. 3, pp. 189-90

Table 4. The impact of neuromarketing on product development

PRODUCT DEVELOPMENT	IMPACT OF NEUROMARKETING
New product introduction into the market	• Product taste, smell and colour • Health/fashion trends • Identification of new target groups.
Product packaging/design	• Logotype position • Colour distribution • Packaging material • Packaging size • Limited edition product range • Smell.
Product distribution	• Position on the shelf • Product positioning • Creating special offers • Smell, music and general impression about the facility • Product availability.

Source: Reynolds, J., 2006. Measurement and Analysis for Marketing. Journal of Targeting, Vol. 14 No. 3, pp. 189-90

Table 5. Limitations of research in neuromarketing

LIMITATION TYPE	SPECIFICATION
Technological limitations	• 7% of test subjects around the world are not suitable for brain testing • Obsolete devices and their noise may cause the subject to give up on testing • Test subjects may provide wrong test results if affected by fear • Large and non-flexible devices • Testing requires medical monitoring • Due to time and financial limitations, a small number of test subjects may undergo testing.
General limitations	• Consumer behaviour cannot be determined in the laboratory • Brain activity cannot be measured without prior consent of the consumer • Ethical issues should not be reduced solely to the field of neuromarketing • Limited precision and accuracy in measuring brain activity.

Source: Mucha, T., 2005. This is your brain on advertising. Business 2.0,35 pp.7-35., Mucha, T., 2005. Why the caveman loves the pitchman,. Business 2.0.,35, pp.9-37.

As evident from the analysed sample, we find technological and general limitations in neuromarketing. It is precisely because of such limitations that we can conclude that neuromarketing is a discipline which cannot be viewed as a separate discipline, but as an integral part of the marketing discipline, to which it may serve as an addition to marketing research.[22]

SCIENTIFIC RESEARCH IN NEUROMARKETINGS

The marketing profession has proved a direct link between the brand of a particular product and the brain. The results of scientific research were so shocking that even the scientists and advertisers started paying attention to the facts they had acquired through research. Moreover, the necessity of knowing how the human brain functions in the moments of purchase decision making has been proven.

"PEPSI PARADOX"

In 2004, the Center for Theoretical Neuroscience at Baylor College of Medicine published the "Read Montague" study, which is one of the earliest published marketing studies. Scientists have found inspiration for the study in the existent promotional campaign by Pepsi (Pepsi Challenge). During their research, they conducted tests on 67 experimental subjects whose brains were scanned after being given a Pepsi and a Coca Cola. Blind study results (after the experimental subjects had been asked which drink they would choose), have shown that one half of experimental would opt for a Coca Cola, and the other half for a Pepsi.

On the other hand, when the experimental subjects were asked to drink a Coca Cola for half an hour, and then take a Pepsi, 75% of experimental subjects concluded that Coca Cola tasted better with respect to Pepsi (25%). However, cumulative results ultimately differed significantly. The research results have proven that consumers will want to buy a Coca Cola regardless of its taste, but solely due to its brand name, while they will buy a Pepsi exclusively for its taste. The study has ultimately proven why Pepsi didn't win the so-called

"Coca - Cola war", because despite the fact that consumers thought that Pepsi tasted better, the emotional attachment of consumers towards the Coca Cola brand is stronger.[23]

"BUYLOGY"

In one of his studies, M. Lindstrom conducted research on the connection between prominent warning labels on cigarette packs ("a cigarette which causes lung cancer") and their interaction among smokers. Research has proven that prominent warnings on cigarette packs do not affect smokers at all. The reason for this lies in the fact that such warning messages have actually stimulated the said part of the brain in smokers (*nucleus accumbens*). Furthermore, they have encouraged smokers to light a cigarette.[24]

"THE AMERICAN IDOL"

M. Lindstrom conducted research on product placement in TV commercials, with the following primary goal: finding out if the viewers remembered a specific logo. In the "American Idol" (2008) TV show, three product brands, such as: Coca Cola, Cingular Wireless and Ford were the subjects of research. All the three companies paid the same amount for advertising in the TV show (26 mil. USD), but Coca Cola was represented with 60%, Cingular Wireless was less represented (although the TV presenter was constantly repeating when addressing the viewers that they could vote by phone if they were users of C.W., with the logo of the company being constantly displayed in the background), while Ford was represented with only 30 seconds during commercial break.

Blind test results obtained before the show have demonstrated that experimental subjects did not remember any extra product in comparison to other products which were advertised before the beginning of the show. At the end of the show, Coca Cola was the most memorable. Research results have demonstrated that being annoyed with Coca Cola commercials has had an impact on suppressing the memory of Ford's advertising messages. The marketing profession has proven that consumers do not remember any of the brands which are not part of the show they are watching.[25]

SUBLIMINAL MESSAGES

The aim of the research was to determine whether subliminal messages (subconscious images) had any impact on the increased consumption of cigarettes. At the beginning, the experimental subjects were shown the pictures which were not related in any way to the cigarette brand (the landscape showing the Wild West in the USA with cowboys and sunset in the desert).

Then scans were made using fMRI, which recorded activity in the part of the brain that is in charge of rewarding, desire and envy. In other words, the study has proven that there are several activities in the centre of the brain for rewarding and desire when the experimental subject is exposed to subliminal images of a well-known brand. The sunset has increased the consumption of cigarettes.[26]

WHAT CAN PR LEARN FROM NEUROMARKETING?

Let us recall the following: the fundamental principles of public relations are based on the three basic elements, such as: 1) to inform the public, 2) to persuade the public, 3) to connect the public with specific community/industry groups (Bernays).

It is common for PR departments not to use all the relevant and available information when publishing an article/ text or the news. In other words, they use only one, the so-called "representative part" of the unit, thinking that this is exactly why their "PR" would achieve the best effect. Although the modern way of life sometimes even imposes this so-called "mental shortcut", the decisions we make under such circumstances are often very primitive, because they are made based on no evidence at all. However, such an isolated piece of information, which advises and/or informs the consumers, can lead you to some really stupid mistakes–because of which, if they are used wisely by the others, you can look ridiculous, and for which you may also be held legally responsible. It used to be enough to rely on the perfect rhetorics (the ancient Greeks).

Moreover, in ancient Babylonians, Persians, Sumerians and Assyrians, public opinion has played an important role in the life of a nation, irrespective of their absolute monarchy's rule[27].

At this point, I would like to mention the names such as: Freud, Le Bon, Levitt, Maslow, Lippmann and Cialdini, without whose contribution modern research and progress would not be possible, but today, in the era of globalisation and technological "boom", it is no longer enough to be: "literate", to have the perfect rhetorics, knowledge or to be familiar with persuasive communication techniques, have a degree or know the statutory legislation in this field!

I will use a quote by N. Turret Edelman: "You don't need to be scientists, but you need to understand the basic principles".

Although public relations are an integral part of marketing, what happens in practice is that usually in small businesses (mostly due to ignorance), public relation departments function as a separate unit with no and/or with poor knowledge about marketing and no knowledge at all about the basics of neuromarketing.

Each year, a traditional congress of NeuroPR experts is held in London, the main task of which is to "communicate more efficiently with consumers using the applied psychology and neuroscience, which is emerging as a new and essential tool of PR".[28]

So, now the key question arises, which is as follows:
What can PR experts learn from neuromarketing?

THE PRINCIPLE OF SCARCITY/ SHORTAGE

The students of the State University of Florida were assigned to assess the quality of food at the canteen, on the campus. Most students rated the food "unsatisfactory". After nine days, another assessment was carried out in which the students completely changed their opinion. What happened?

Did the quality of the food improve? No, it didn't. "Something" happened which forced the students not only to change their opinion, but also to like the food at the canteen even more than they did previously! Let us remember that the quality of the food did not change at all.

However, its availability did change. On the day of testing, students were told that due to a fire, they would not be able to eat at the canteen. The technical term is "the principle of scarcity/shortage"[29]. What is exactly "the principle of scarcity" and how is it connected to PR?

The experimental and scientific studies have proven that the loss/losses can trigger an emotion which is even twice as powerful as the gain/gains. The application of PR: Now when you are familiar with this essential fact, in order for you to trigger a specific reaction in consumers, do not imply the following message: for example: "If you do that, you will save €100", but make the following formulation: "save €100 on buying _____, but if you don't do this, you will lose a discount of € _____"[30]

THE PRINCIPLE OF SIMILARITY

Individuals tend to identify themselves with people who are similar to themselves. The application of PR: the principle of "similarity" is mostly used when you wish to deploy large groups of people. In other words, if you wish to gather together a multitude of people for a specific reason, do not use the proclamation of "the cause and the effect", since you can do this in the following way, as well, by stating: "7 out of 10 people are concerned about this situation"[31]

THE PRINCIPLE OF ARGUMENTATION

Studies have shown that today's consumers are aware, and are looking for argumentation/facts/evidence in the statements. The application of PR: Usually, when argumentation is missing, individual PR practitioners make use of emotional appeals in consumers in order to create a diversion.

Such a *modus operandi* will not only result in a PR effect of poor quality, but it is not ethical, either. Moreover, any statement or claim must be substantiated by a bill, because otherwise you have committed an offense. The author's recommendation is the following: emotional appeals may be used solely to signify an arguable claim. A high-quality implementation always produces high-quality results!

However, it is very important to understand which are the advantages that we can "take on" from neuroscience, and apply them in our business?

Toni Muzi Falconi (an international PR expert, NY University) explains as follows: "I believe that many scientists and experts are only beginning to realise that the consumers' opinion is much less correlated to their behaviour than 10 or 15 years ago. If this hypothesis is only partially true, this means that we (as a marketing, political and social industry) should focus our attention on a better understanding of our behaviour than our opinion. And this certainly makes it necessary to revise our auditory processes through an improved knowledge of psychology and neuroscience..."

Although neuroscience studies the methodology and patterns of human behaviour, neuromarkreting studies the interaction between behaviour and decision making. The knowledge of psychology is essential, and most PR experts know the basics of persuasive communication. Public relations have a significant impact on the public, and are responsible for the ultimate outcome they have achieved by means of their proclamation in public.

However, regardless of the whole array of both simple and sophisticated techniques you can learn, you must never forget the most important principle: the ethical principle, because this very principle, together with our ability to process information, is what makes us a dominant species on the planet. Still though, our capacity is limited. Sometimes, due to a lack of will, time, strength, or if we are stressed, we are not able to analyse the situation well. If we make decisions in such situations, we take a very primitive, though necessary, approach of reducing the evidence[32].

Because of this very discouraging, though essential, fact, it is no longer enough to know the traditional techniques and tools of PR. Therefore, we must ask ourselves the following: what type of communication will provide the strongest response or produce the most positive feedback from consumers?[33]

If used properly, by following the example of the best world practice, contained within ethical standards, neuromarketing will improve the strategic business value of public relations. Do not forget the following:

"MAXIMA EX NIHILO NASCITUR HISTORIA"
–the greatest story arises out of nothing!

CHAPTER 3

MARKETING WAR TACTICS

Key topics covered by this chapter

- ✓ Strategic Marketing – Why do I need this?

- ✓ Large companies fail and the small ones thrive?!

- ✓ Permission Marketing – What is that?

- ✓ E-mail Marketing is Dead!

MARKETING WAR TACTICS

In the year 500 B.C. Sun Tzu, the great military strategist of the ancient China, wrote the treatise entitled "The Art of War". From today's perspective, most of his approaches could be deemed barbaric, but his views, as well as the very attitudes about the strategy, are still relevant today, both for military commanders and entrepreneurs. They have one goal only: to find out how to defeat "the enemy".

Sun Tzu's treatise is based on the psychological hypothesis stating that the highest form of warfare is to attack the strategy itself with the aim of submitting or forcing the adversary into submission, but without entering the battle! Hence the saying: "Know your enemy, know yourself, and you need not fear the result of a hundred battles. The one who knows himself, but does not know his enemy, will achieve the same number of victories and defeats. The one who does not know himself nor his enemy will suffer defeat in each battle".

Today there are various military strategies in the market on how to defeat the enemy (in our case, the competitors), which are used in the world of business: lateral strategies, environmental strategies, siege strategies, frontal assault, even *guerilla* marketing tactics. However, the selection of any of the strategies aimed at gaining competitive advantage in the market, must be in accordance with the law and legal regulations. Although some people find it "appealing" to use the so-called "unlawful rules of market competition", and thus to unfairly acquire the competitive advantage, such activities may send you to prison, pose a threat to your publicity, make you lose "goodwill" (the value of the company which is estimated based on its reputation), as well as revenue. Therefore, there is a growing need for competitive intelligence in business. It rests on the premiss which concerns the way in which to make the entire organisation more concrete with respect to its shareholders, customers, competitors, distributors, technology, macroeconomic situation in the market etc. In other words, competitive intelligence is an indispensable tool in strategic marketing planning. It is also worth mentioning that competitive intelligence is an ethical and completely legal method of data collection, as opposed to industrial espionage which represents a completely illegal form of business operation. The former is the procedure which is implemented with the purpose of teaching us how to use plenty of data available to collect quality data, synthesise them and turn them into useful information that we will be able to use in our future business decision making. You might think that collecting information on competitors matches treasure hunt, or that you will have to go a long way in order to find just a few grains of gold which make the task worthwhile. Sometimes, even the best analysts, searching for "gold", will find a lot of "gloss", but with the help of the techniques listed below and experience, the risk of failure will be minimised. Therefore, let's go in search of information.

First of all, we need to identify your competitors:

a. companies which offer the same products or services

b. companies which offer similar products or services

c. companies which may offer the same or similar products and services in the future

d. companies which may reduce the need for our products and services.

When you get to know who your competitors are, you will be able to predict their strategic moves, take advantage of their weaknesses, and undermine their advantages!

Now you need to answer the following questions:

a. What do we need to find out? /goals/

b. What do we already know? /facts/

c. Why do we need to know that? /planning/

d. Until when do we need to find this out? /planning/

e. What are we going to do with all the data we have collected? /synthesis of information/

f. How much will it cost us to obtain all this information? / plans/

g. How much will it cost us if we do not obtain this information?

Nowadays, there is a great wealth of information available on the Internet. You must know that there is information your competitors don't mind if you see it, and there is information your competitors hope you won't see. In both cases, you need to analyse all the information starting from the following: press release, announcements published on your company's website, analytical reports, annual newsletters etc.

Don't count your chickens before they are hatched!

Through systematic planning, research, as well as the collection, analysis and dissemination of the obtained information, you will be able to understand and know your competitor in terms of the following:

— his way of thinking

— his advantages (strengths)

— his weaknesses

— his vulnerable side

— where you can attack him, and

— the risk you will bear if you take an inferior attitude.

Of course, it's in the interest of the competitor to hide crucial information which may refer to the following: the difference between profit and loss, the expansion of business activity, or the company's bankruptcy. It is essential for the company's survival to identify such information, especially in today's turbulent times.

Let's take a look at the following example:

You are the owner of a company engaged in wholesale of bicycle parts. Your company is currently paying €50 for the purchase price of the parts which it then sells to resellers for €150, so that the final price of your bicycle parts reaches the retail price amounting to €250. Your company is currently holding a market share of 10 %, with its revenue amounting to €50 per bicycle. Your competitor orders those same items from China for €25, thus making a profit of €75 per bicycle. Should your company propose a discount of €25 for each product purchased?

This would reduce the profit for each bicycle by €25, and even if you doubled your sales volume, you would still achieve the same net pofit. In a competitive analysis, you need to assume what your competitor is going to do. Suppose that the competitor reduces his price. In that case, your company would still retain the market share of 10 % and would lose half of its profit, while the competitor would lose 1/3 of the net profit. However, what would happen if your competitor offered a discount of €50? He would still be making a profit of €25 per bicycle, but your company would not operate anymore. This is one of the striking examples which show that it is of vital strategic importance for each company to know the techniques and tools of competitive intelligence. By doing so, managers will be able to do the following: a) improve the quality of products and services, b) understand how necessary it is for the company to implement strategic planning, and c) understand the vital importance of marketing.

There are several commonly used tools of competitive intelligence (ranging from *benchmarking,* scenario planning and financial forensics to the popular war game), but it is important to emphasise its importance and relevance in preventing and diversifying the risk of a potential failure (whether it be a new acquisition of a company or the introduction of a new product on the market), as well as in improving your current position on the market in comparison to competitors.[34]

LARGE COMPANIES FAIL AND THE SMALL ONES THRIVE?

Formerly, those same companies used to base their domination on the market on economies of scale. Today, however, this is not an advantage anymore. Changes in technology, financial market, distribution channels and access to information, have led to fundamental changes on the market. Today, it is not sufficient to be a large company with a name (brand) anymore. It is important to manage changes, now more than ever.

Although these techniques cannot predict the future of our company with absolute certainty, by evaluating the past we can extrapolate future trends of our business. The real value of competitive intelligence is that it will provide answers to managers' questions relating to what a competitor is going to do, not to what he has done![35]

PERMISSION MARKETING- WHAT IS THAT?

"Permission marketing" is turning strangers into friends and friends into loyal customers.
(-Seth Godin)

In the time of Facebook, Twitter, and other social networks and media, in the time of e-books, Internet marketing, direct marketing and interactive marketing communication, in the time of digital products (e-services), it is very useful to know the techniques and tools of "Permission Marketing", known also as "Marketing with permission". In the past, when the pace of life was slower, less stressful, and when the advertising market had not yet reached the saturation point, we did not mind the so-called "intrusion advertising", such as a dishwashing liquid ad campaign that would make us stop watching our favourite TV show.

We did not mind if we received a phone call from a cookware seller who interrupted us during a pleasant family gathering, because he wanted to arrange a cookware set presentation. However, times have changed, and the techniques and tools of mass marketing have still been used today for distinctive purposes, with the aim of implementing company' strategies. Companies are increasingly making efforts to win the customer loyalty towards a specific brand/product and to gain customer trust. For this very reason, many advertisers follow the examples of "the big fish", without them even realising that this is a special type of techniques of "Permission Marketing".

"Permission marketing is the practice of marketing to consumers only after having received their permission. It is a tool used by companies to distinguish themselves among others and build customer loyalty" (Kotler, Keller: Marketing Management, 12th ed.).

The originator of this technique is Seth Godin, who claims that the technique represents a kind of challenge for the marketing profession, since companies need to convince consumers in order to get their attention, respect their wishes, and transmit promotional messages only when the customers want this. In this way, customers associate themselves more with the product brand and participate in creating enterprise value, while the manufacturers get to know the habits and needs of their customers better.

Do you remember how many "SPAM" messages you have received in your e-mail inbox?![36]

E-MAIL MARKETING IS DEAD!

During the first generation of *e-mail* marketing, companies were sending their promotional materials to several different *e-mail* addresses on a massive scale, with their *e-mails* ultimately ending up among "junk mail", and their *e-mail* addresses were "blacklisted". In the long run, their *e-mails* were "sent and forgotten", and they were mostly "irrelevant to the recipient". However, many companies are doing this still today following the example of bad practice, mostly due to ignorance. Although "Permission Marketing" belongs to the second generation of *e-mail* marketing, the knowledge of it is becoming ever more important. Not only for the purpose of an enhanced involvement of customers with the product/brand/company, but for the purpose of getting familiar with legislation as well, where this area of marketing is fully regulated by law.

As you can see, *e-mail* marketing appears to be a good choice: a) faster response times, b) low price, c) targetedness. However, if we take a look at the studies, we will see that as much as 95 % of the *e-mail* marketing communication fails, and that 98 % of companies/enterprises use *e-mail* marketing without a clear goal/vision (Fokus Integrated; M. L. Nielsen, 2008).

In most cases, customers' requests are ignored, such as: "Don't send me offers from Dubai, since I am staying there", or "Don't provide me with cost savings on your products if you don't deliver them by post". How is permission-based *e-mail* marketing to be used properly? First of all, ask yourself the following question: "What is your true value?", "What is it that you offer that I could be interested in?". On most *web* sites, you will notice the following content: "Subscribe to our *newsletter*". Such a formulation of a sentence is not your powerful sales weapon, isn't it? Try, for example, with this one: "Be the first one to find out about our...".

Ask yourself the following question: "If customers subscribe to my *newsletter*, what are they actually buying"? YOUR PROMISES! Be sure not to forget this, because you have a professional, moral and legal obligation to fulfill them as well!

What do you have to do????

1. Make a syndication (bring the content where users are located, instead of attracting them to your website);

2. Offer a text to your buyer which will provide him with information about the product/service (in this way you will receive direct feedback);

3. Use the Internet for differentitation purposes (everything is clear here J;

4. Create new form of your offer, and offer high-quality "additional content" (read the chapter on the "fried egg strategy");

5. Use reintermediation (introducing new intermediators who act as links between manufacturers and consumers).[37]

"The permission you have received from your customers is like getting to know someone on a date. You don't want to start a conversation with a request for the sales of your products and services. You want to deserve this right, over time."[38]

CHAPTER 4

WHAT ARE PRODUCT LABELS
HIDING FROM US?

Key topics covered by this chapter

✓ Greenwashing

✓ Research, research, what does it tell us?

✓ Story of my life: "Naked Juice" & "Natural

✓ Semantic traps

✓ How to interpret hidden economic indicators?!

✓ The interpretation of figures in economics

✓ Percentage scores

✓ Growth rates

✓ Seasonality

✓ The measuring of economic activity

WHAT ARE PRODUCT LABELS HIDING FROM US?

GREENWASHING

Have you ever heard the term: "greenwashing"? The etymology of the word is a combination of the lexemes *green* and *whitewashing* (washing or painting in a literary or figurative sense), with the term "green" representing a symbol of the natural environment and the need for its conservation. The originator of the term is J. Westerveld, who used it for the first time in 1986 in his essay regarding the hotel industry's practice, in which he advocated the placing of placards in each hotel room promoting reuse of towels, supposedly to "save the natural environment" (op. cit. Wikipedia). The term is used today in professional marketing practice to bring attention to the fact that a specific PR activity is accompanied by "greenwashing", which means the following: the term "green marketing" implies the placing of products and services onto the market which are not harmful to the environment or human health, and are tested and safe for use. Such statements must be true and verifiable.

All the other claims which are too general, vague, broad etc., leading customers to wrong conclusions, are called "greenwashing" by experts. Have you ever noticed the following declarations on products, such as "dermatologically tested", "clinically proven", "not tested on animals", "energetically efficient"? I truly believe that you have, more than once.

These are only some of the striking examples of "greenwashing".[39]

RESEARCH, RESEARCH, – WHAT DOES IT TELL US?

According to research data from Portland State University, Oregon Physicians for Social Responsibility: "How corporations and the media disseminate environmental misinformation", it has been observed that the average American spends 900 hours a year in school, and 1,500 hours a year watching TV. In other words, by the age of 65, the average American will have spent 9 years watching TV! Now, if we take a look at research data published in the most recent Greenwashing Report[40] journal published by TerraChoice, an independent organisation engaged in the activity which is a combination of science and environmental marketing, the analysis of 1,000 various products most commonly used by consumers, has showed the following: in 2010, the products which were advertised as "green" have shown an increase of 73% compared to the advertising of products with the same significant characteristics in 2009 companies with experience in "greenwashing" have been investing in improving the characteristics of their products, and are recording an increase in their relevant certifications unfortunately, there has been an increase in false statements leading consumers to wrong conclusions (the analysis was conducted using ISO 14024 standard guidelines) an increase of 577 % has been observed in demand for "BPA free" products (products which do not contain harmful Bisphenol A), consequently leading to an increase of 2,550 % in the range of products containing false and unfounded statements.

Do you decide about the quality and safety of a specific product based on the previously generated perception of its brand (registered trademark)? In most cases, the answer is: "YES". In order to gain a competitive advantage over the competitors, we can use "green marketing". However, this is where the risk of "greenwashing" lies, the existence of which creates distrust in the proclamation of "green marketing". For this very reason, you must take heed of some of the most frequent warning signs of "greenwashing"[41]

Partial truth

One of the examples of highlighting partial truth on a product is highlighting the claim on the packaging that, for example, in manufacturing the product 52 % of the recycled paper was used. This claim is partially true since it is not mentioned in what way the remaining 48 % of it was produced.

Non-provable claims

In accordance with the applicable laws in some countries, highlighting of claims which are not provable and can mislead consumers is prohibited and unlawful. The group of claims which are non-provable, regardless of whether such claims appear in the form of an image (symbol) or text, and/or a combination of the two, which cannot be supported by a certificate or some other evidence, includes the claims such as "dermatologically tested", "clinically proven", "not tested on animals", with the given claim not containing the following information: "Who does the testing of the given product?", "Where was the product tested?", "How was it tested?", "Are there any test reports available?" etc. In other words, all these given claims have been highlighted, but there is no evidence to support them.[42]

Vague claims

An example of claims highlighted as vague on products are claims such as "chemical free" (the claim is considered vague as it is not explicitly stated which are the chemicals that the product contains that are hazardous to health). Actually, everything that surrounds us is composed of chemical compounds. The claim such as "natural product" has been officially classified into the vague claim category since lead, arsenic, and uranium are found in nature as toxic and hazardous to health, although the afore-mentioned claim should be proclaiming something good.[43]

Highlighting irrelevant claims

You must have taken a product containing claims which is irrelevant to consumers more than once, with the purpose of selecting a product which is considered less harmful to the environment and human health. This refers to the statements which are highlighted on the product, claiming that the product does not contain specific compounds that represent the main causes of ozone layer depletion.[44]

Misleading/false claims

Now, you must be wondering why the companies/reputable and recognised brands are doing this? According to the latest research data[45], potential reasons have been identified, which are as follows:

NAIVETY

SLOPPINESS

OPPORTUNITY/INCREASING DEMAND

MISTAKE

LYING DELIBERATELY

In December 2005, the NY Times reported that corporations such as Ford, Exxon, Mobile, BP and General Electric would invest most of their promotion budget in "greenwashing". In order for us to be able to make a comparative overview in relation to the year 2010, quantitatively, we can conclude that in the latest research[46], based on 9022 online interviews held in Australia, Brazil, China, Germany, India, USA, and UK, in the period from February 27th to March 24th, 2010:

- 60 % of key customers stated (on a sample taken across a wide geographic region including the said countries) that they wanted to purchase products from the companies that cared about the environment
- customers expect that companies which take care about the environment actively participate in environmental initiatives
- despite the recession, 30 % of shoppers are planning to spend more money on purchasing products which are considered to be "green", and this applies in particular to developing countries. We are aware of the fact that the advertising proclaiming the so-called "green products" on the market increases the consumers' interest, and thus also the demand for such products, as well as the sales coefficient.

Moreover, according to published research data, we can confirm that shoppers want quality products, and they give priority to the products which are safe for the environment and for human health.

On the other hand, the same data point to the fact that there is an increase in promotions of those same products through the so-called "greenwashing" due to the following: "naivety, slopiness, seizing an opportunity to make a profit, mistake and lying deliberately". Only owing to hard work and high-quality business operation will we be able to retain our position on the market in the long run. Therefore, one should always give priority to organisation over improvisation.

Try answering the question which is apparently so simple, and it is as follows:

"Please, give all the reasons why a consumer should choose your very product".

You might be surprised at the answers you will receive.

STORY OF MY LIFE:
"NAKED JUICE" AND "NATURAL"

You have all heard about PepsiCo Inc. However, have you ever drunk Naked juice and Natural? This is an impressive example of how even large businesses (whether deliberately or by accident) are misleading consumers. I bring you a part of the report published on their official website: www.leanwashingindex.com. These are just a few of the basic guidelines that each company should follow. *Recently, PepsiCo Inc. announced that it would no longer label its Naked juices as being "all natural," after a litigation claim that the drinks clearly contained non-natural ingredients. In light of this, we wondered what would happen to the word "natural" in food marketing. We turned to Bruce Bradley, a Leanwashing Index advisory panel member, to help us sort out what this could mean for the word "natural" in marketing.*

Q: "How should "natural" be defined when it's used by advertisers?

A: I think "natural" should be defined in line with what consumers believe the word actually means. But what I think will happen is slightly different.

Q: How do you think "natural" should be defined?

A: "Natural" should only be used to describe products that use ingredients that come from nature and are minimally processed. What does "minimally processed" mean? For example, a stevia leaf is natural. Flavour extracted from that stevia leaf by crushing it and soaking it and then concentrating that liquid is natural. But when stevia leaves are processed through some 40-plus-step patented process that includes the use of acetone, methanol, ethanol, acetonitrile and isopropanol, then that's no longer natural. Yet within today's system of no rules, Truvia (a sweetener in part derived from stevia leaves) calls itself "natural."

Q: Will the government step in and regulate the use of "natural" in advertising?

A: I think the Food and Drug Administration is going to be forced to define "natural." Consumers are frustrated, manufacturers don't like to get sued, and the courts are asking the FDA for direction. So I'm pretty confident we will get a definition for "natural" in the next year or so.

Q: Will that cut down on the use of "natural" in leanwashing?

A: I'm very sceptical that the definition the FDA comes up with will be meaningful or in line with what consumers' believe "natural" means. Given the influence that the food industry has with the FDA, it's very likely that the definition we end up with will have many loopholes.

Q: Will a legal definition of "natural" be effective in reducing leanwashing, even with the loopholes?

A: No matter what definition the FDA ultimately comes up with, it will likely reduce the abuse of the term "natural" to some extent. However, I don't expect the FDA will make a ruling that is truly in sync with what consumers believe is "natural," so the term is likely to remain quite misleading to an average person.

Q: In addition to FDA action, what are some of the best ways to hold companies accountable for misusing the word "natural"?

A: Within our current system, there really aren't many ways to hold companies accountable other than consumers calling them out on sites like the Leanwashing Index or via other social media. If and when the FDA does define the term "natural", taking companies to court will only work if they violate the definition established by the FDA."[47]

SEMANTIC TRAPS

Alchemists had their "lapis philosophorum", better known as the "philosopher's stone", and what do you have?

Each of us uses the term "money" daily for several different purposes. We use it as a synonym for income: "to make money", and as a synonym for wealth: "he has got a lot of money." In economics, you must be very careful when using the afore-said terms as their meaning and their usage in a linguistic and economic sense can have dual, or even completely different meanings. So, first things first:

INCOME – income represents your weekly, monthly or annual earnings (salary), as well as everything you have earned from part-time work (service contracts, author's royalties contracts etc.), including interest rates and dividends. Income is always measured per time unit, and that is why we call it a "flow variable". When journalists asked J. Paul Getty on one occasion what was the amount of his income, he replied: "1,000 dollars." However, what the journalists were not able to interpret in economic terms (per time unit, in this case), and was not mentioned, was actually the following: "1,000 dollars per minute".

WEALTH – what is meant here is financial wealth, which includes the total value of all your financial assets minus your current liabilities. At this point, it is worth mentioning that, unlike income, wealth is a variable of state, not a flow variable. In other words, financial wealth (assets) is estimated at a given point in time.

MONEY – all the financial assets which can be used for purchasing goods and services, is called "money". The money includes the following: cash, cheques, various deposits etc.

Money = value. You must take into consideration the fact that one may, for example, have significant wealth, but keep small amounts of cash or have a high salary, but still have a modest positive balance on his current account.

INVESTMENT – the term is frequently used by economists in communication science, particularly when it comes to purchasing new goods (ranging from machines to office buildings). However, when you wish to talk about the purchase of stock, it is to be called: "financial investment".

Consider the following method you should use in order to be able to express yourself accurately in economic terms. It is wrong to say: "Jack earns a lot of money" – but rather: "Jack earns a substantial income." It is also wrong to say: "Jill has got a lot of money" – but you should rather say the following: "Jill is very rich". Although this mini-course in avoiding semantic traps seems insignificant, this was an interesting example of common mistakes in word choice and perception.

If we get these seemingly simple terms wrong, imagine how difficult it is to generate an economically valuable and cost-effective perception inside the mind of consumers and to position oneself on the market?![48]

HOW TO INTERPRET HIDDEN ECONOMIC INDICATORS?!

*Are we really supposed to believe that "Forrest Gump"
was a failure?*

You have just found out on the news that bond market is soaring. Does this mean that interest rates will decrease, thus making the purchasing of a new computer easier than before? Does this indicate an early recovery of the economy, and is it now the right time to construct a new building?

Is it smarter to access new funds through bond emission, or to seek a loan from your home bank? However, if you are an importer and you import goods from abroad, should you be worried about the fact that the cost of the services of the supplier from whom you import goods has increased?

This is just another striking example of how much a single piece of information may have a direct impact not only on our entire economy but on our daily life, as well. It goes without saying that such information causally affects the operating profit of your company, as well as the production of goods and the providing of services. Back in 1970, George Akerlof, Nobel laureate, in his famous article "The Market for Lemons: Quality Uncertainty and the Market Mechanism[49] he used colourful imagery to present the problem of negative data selection and its impact on the used car market, on the example of the purchase of a damaged vehicle. Take a look at the following example: at the heart of the film industry, the accounting practice has gained a bad reputation. Along with its bad reputation, it has also earned the appellative "Hollywood accounting". Namely, it has been a common practice for the film industry to keep double-entry bookkeeping. One bookkeeping system is run in accordance with the generally accepted accounting standards and is used by the Board of Directors and by shareholders for reporting of profit. The other form of bookkeeping, popularly called "contract bookkeeping", is used to pay a percentage of the "net profit" to actors, directors, screenwriters, and all the other contractual parties. However, if some film studios are driven by the so-called "moral hazard" in minimising "net profit" upon payment, in practice it is rarely a positive one.

This brings us to our question:
"Was Forrest Gump a failure?"

The film "Forrest Gump" made a profit of 600 million dollars, along with films "Batman", "J. F. K", and "Coming to America", but it did not generate any profit to the Paramount Pictures film studio. Are we really supposed to believe that "Forrest Gump" was a failure?

THE INTERPRETATION OF FIGURES IN ECONOMICS

All the politicians share a common interest, which is to achieve the fastest economic growth rate, the largest drop in unemployment rate, and the lowest inflation rate. However, you must be wondering how you should interpret such claims. The aim of this chapter is to teach you how to read the figures, identify the ones which are most relevant among numerous figures published in the media, and to determine what are these figures supposed to mean, without previous knowledge of economics, statistics, and arithmetics.

Do you know why it is important to know how to interpret the figures in economics?

Here are some of the examples:

You may wish to do the following:

a. obtain the highest financial return on the invested capital

b. decide whether it was the right time to undertake a new investment project or to conquer new markets

c. assess the government's economic policies for the purpose of taking over new companies

d. predict market conditions in order for you to be able to protect your price policy from unexpected impacts on time, or you just wish to make a comparison with other countries, achieve a better understanding of the way in which the economy as a whole operates.

Herbert Hoover, a former US president, once said: "Please find me a one-armed economist so we will not always hear: on the other hand… ". In order for you to be able to avoid this, in this chapter, we will learn how to interpret some of the main economic indicators because it is almost impossible to present all the economic agents of analysis in a short summary. When interpreting figures in economics, you should be able to tell the difference between the actual effects of inflation and actual changes in the economic activity.

There are three basic indicators, which are as follows:

1. quantity (for example, a tonne of steel)

2. value (for example, the market value of steel)

3. price (for example, the market value of 1 tonne of steel).

Now, when you know this, it is important for you to remember the following:

• value, current price or nominal price (current selling price) and nominal conditions include the cost of inflation,

• as well whereas

• quantity, constant price, the actual price and actual conditions exclude any impact of inflation.

Why is this important? I will show you on a stunning example the following complication which may lead you to a completely wrong conclusion: if we observe the three afore-mentioned indicators, their interrelation looks like this: quantity x price = value. Now, let us assume, for example, that the quantity of steel manufactured each year is evaluated according to the actual price, let us say, according to the price for the year 2011. The result is the following: an *output* indicator of the price for the year 2011. However, such steel production series is expressed in monetary units, which is an indicator of quantity, not a price indicator. And thus we arrive at the wrong interpretation because such a representation actually provides information on changes in quantity, not on changes in price.[50]

PERCENTAGE SCORES

Another most common mistake in interpreting figures in economics includes percentage scores. Percentage scores do not have any similarity with changes in percentage. For example, financial experts use minor changes in interest rate or exchange rate. For the purpose of making a more simple calculation, 1 %, i.e., 1 percentage score was divided into 100 base scores. 1 base score = 0,01 %, 100 base scores = 1,00 %. Please observe the following example: You have arranged a bank loan. However, after some time the interest rate increased from 10 % to 13 %. Some people may conclude that actually, the interest rate increased by 3 % in total. However, the interest rate actually increased by 30 %! How is this possible? If the interest rate increased from 10 % to 13 %, then it increased by 3 percentage scores or three units (3:10x100), which ultimately leads to an overall increase of 30 %. You can calculate the change in the inflation rate using the same method.

GROWTH RATES

When calculating growth rates, American economists usually concentrate on growth rates expressed on an annual basis. Although this may reduce the time significantly, since you don't need to make a comparison of monthly and quarterly changes, but unfortunately this may lead you astray. Many economic figures vary from month to month, and extraordinary market fluctuations inflate overall growth rates which are expressed on an annual basis. In other words, a monthly change of just 0,1 %, increases the overall 1,2 %, to the amount brought down to the total annual value.

Observe the following example: If consumer expenditure grows at a rate of 1 % per month, how much will it grow at the end of the year? 12 %? No. The expenditure will increase by 12,7 %! How come? If we take, for example, the fact that each monthly expenditure has increased by 1 % with respect to the previous month (let us not forget that each percentage increase contains several bases), we may conclude that an annual 12,7 % is the same as a monthly 1 % increase.[51]

SEASONALITY

Several economic figures follow a seasonal pattern which is constantly repeated every year. For example, in winter there is an increase in electricity used, as well as the price of seasonal food, while in summer there is an increase in the sales of sunglasses, and industrial production is declining due to the holiday season. It is worth mentioning that several economic figures have been adjusted on a seasonal basis for the purpose of making the interpretation easier, which in itself brings certain faults that may lead you to wrong interpretation and wrong conclusions. For example, since the quantity of the energy consumed increases in winter for an amount which is larger than the amount that is expected according to the seasonal adjustment, one may misinterpret these figures as an increase in the energy consumption. Or, since most construction workers cannot work in winter with the usual amount which is smaller that the one expected, these figures may be misinterpreted as an increase in unemployment rate.

Namely, the seasonal adjustment is a very simple numerical method used in economics which is used for the adjustment of approximate data for the observed seasonal pattern. You can calculate this for yourself very easily. For example, if the sales of swimwear or the *output* in June usually amounts to 75 % of the monthly average, the seasonal adjustment means that you should divide all the observed figures for June by 75 %, and you will obtain the final calculation for this specific month.

However, since seasonality is subject to minor deviations, you need to examine a number of data, form your own opinion on the trend, and you should not exclude it until you have obtained a clear confirmation that the trend is changing.[52]

THE MEASURING OF ECONOMIC ACTIVITY

Each economic activity can be measured in three different, though equally valuable ways such as GDP (Gross Domestic Product), GNP (Gross National Product) and NNI (Net National Income). Today, all major countries use GDP as the main measure for calculating economic activity. In an ideal situation, measures for *output*, expenditure, and income would be the same. However, due to a difference in the time of the publishing of transactions, "grey economy" and inevitable problems in data collection, differences occur in these three measures, which usually vary from 1 to 2 % of GDP. For this reason, the safest approach is to take the average of all the three measures as an indicator of general trends in the economy. The measure of income is another useful basis used for predicting inflation.

Why is this important? For example, there is a nominal growth in GDP of 13 % and an inflation rate of 10 %, resulting in the actual overall growth in GDP of 3 %. However, if the inflation rate is higher, for example, if it amounts to 11 %, that the actual GDP growth has halved to 2 %. Unfortunately, the inflation rate can never be accurately predicted, which brings uncertainty as a direct consequence, and causally affects investment as a whole.

For this very purpose, the price stabilisation represents the main objective of central banks, since it directly affects income redistribution, as well. The annual inflation rate from 0 to 3 % is usually considered a good inflation rate. If you notice a double-digit percentage, this is bad news. It indicates deflation and usually a decline in economic activity.[53]

Finally, I leave you with the thought that 2+2=5!

CHAPTER **5**

"GIVE AND TAKE"...AND TAKE SOME MORE!

Key topics covered by this chapter

✓ The "Door-in-the-face" technique!

✓ How to market products in times of crisis?!

✓ Have you heard the scientific term the "Butterfly effect"?

✓ Between order and chaos!

✓ Anticipatory Crisis Management- Whaat??

"GIVE AND TAKE"...AND TAKE SOME MORE!

How many times did it happen to you that you bought some product although you should have bought something completely different? It occurred to me so many times! J Do you think this is a coincidence? No, this is not a technique of neuromarketing, but a technique used in psychology which is called the "door-in-the-face" technique.[54]

THE "DOOR-IN-THE-FACE" TECHNIQUE!

Let us suppose that you want me to agree to one of your requests! How are you going to do that??? First of all, you will ask me to do you a bigger favour that you know in advance I would not accept, and after I do reject it, you will make a request to me that you wished to make in the first place. If you satisfied the condition of a cleverly structured request, I will most likely regard your request as a concession and I should feel obliged to return the favour, that is, I will be willing to respond to your request. How can we apply this to products?

For example, I want to sell chocolate bars. Today, there are so many different chocolate brands in the market, and I have a new chocolate brand that has not been positioned yet but do not have sufficient resources to invest in marketing. Therefore, I will use the said technique in the following way: first of all, I will offer you the product I already know that you will refuse in 90 percent of cases. For example, maybe some cinema tickets which cost €5 – you will refuse, and then I will offer you a chocolate bar the cost of which is €0,70 and you will probably buy it! If you have worked or work in sales, the first thing they have taught you was that, when the buyer refuses to buy your product, you ask him or her to give you a list of the names of people that you believe would be interested in purchasing this product.

Research has shown that, when this technique is used during the presentation of a certain product, and when buyers purchase a specific product, in our case this is a chocolate bar, they don't hesitate to write down a list of their friends/acquaintances/colleagues/relatives who might be interested in purchasing the specific product. [55]

As we mentioned earlier, this technique is applied provided that there is reciprocity. We also mentioned other factors and the principle of perceptual contrast.[56]

How does this technique work at the store? This technique is reflected in the implementation of the so-called "a-big-small-request" principle, which may be seen in the stores that offer the so-called "high quality" products. Namely, the buyer is always shown first the product which belongs in the "deluxe" category – (meaning "the most expensive one, the best one, the one of the highest quality"). If the buyer purchases the product, this represents "the topping on the cake", which is the store. However, if the buyer refuses to purchase the product, the shop assistant will immediately offer him or her an alternative product at a much more affordable price.[57] Sounds familiar??! ☺

In order for you to be able to see the evidence of the effectiveness of the application of this technique, I am sharing with you the report published in the Journal of Sales Management that was published in the Consumer Reports Magazine[58] without comment: "if you owned a pool table store, which one would you advertise –the $329 model or the one worth $3,000? You will probably promote the less expensive model hoping that you will be able to offer your customers the more expensive one when he or she comes over to your store. However, G. Warren Kelley, the new director of business marketing in Brunswick, claims that in this way you will make the wrong move. In order to prove this, Kelley points to the sales data of a typical store...In the course of the first week, the buyers...were shown the least expensive models...and then they were offered more expensive ones, as is usually done. In that week pool tables were sold at an average price of $550... However, in the course of the second week, the buyers....were immediately accompanied to the table worth $3,000, regardless of what they wanted to see...and then they were shown the rest of the product line in descending order with respect to the price and quality. The result of such a strategy was the sales of pool tables at an average price of $1,000." ("Quote", 1975, p. 62).

HOW TO MARKET PRODUCTS IN TIMES OF CRISIS?!

"Artis aurifera quam chemiam vocat"- this is the title of the book published 400 years ago with the original title in Latin. The English translation of the book is "On the art of gold production which we call chemistry". The plot of the book reveals the efforts of chemists in earlier centuries who have been nicknamed "alchemists" because they discovered the way in which to transform base metals into precious ones, that is, the way in which to produce gold?! The alchemists were aware of the fact that the so-called "natural materials" (metals) could not be produced naturally, but could be modified. Since their experiments would always fail, the alchemists made it their goal to find the so-called "mysterious force", that is some sort of admixture which could transmute base metal into precious metal – or more precisely, the gold.

This so-called "mysterious force" that was sought by scholars for so many centuries without them being able to find it to this day, is better known as the "philosopher's stone", called by scientists "lapis philosophorum". Why is "philosopher's stone" important? Well, it is only with the help of this stone that it is possible to perform "transmutation".

To this day, the situation in the market has not changed significantly. We are well aware of the fact that, in the times of recession, the market demand for the majority of products and services has decreased with respect to the one in the period of growth, and today we definitely need the "philosopher's stone" that will manage to position the company in a turbulent market. What does the term "positioning" exactly mean?

The positioning of a company refers to the selling of the products and services consumers expect to get. In order for us to be able to achieve this, we need to adjust our "philosopher's stone", namely all marketing activities (the entire marketing mix) to consumers' expectations.

We should make decisions on positioning, and in the times of recession, in particular, based on market research results. Since there are several different techniques or more complex procedures which are implemented in the processing of the data obtained by means of market research, it is important to clearly define one's goals.[59]

First of all, you should ask yourself the following question: "Which are the competitive advantages you wish to promote, and what is the way in which you are going to diversify your portfolio in the market in comparison with other products?"

According to Kotler et. al. (1996, 425.) in order for you to be able to answer the afore-mentioned questions, please make sure that you have met the following criteria:[60]

IMPORTANCE: distinctive advantage delivers a high value to target customers.

PARTICULARITY: other competitors do not offer such distinctive advantage.

SUPERIORITY: your distinctive advantage is significantly superior in comparison to the other methods that consumers take into consideration in order to achieve the same benefit.

COMMUNICATIVENESS: distinctive advantage can be emphasised and is visible to consumers.

UNIQUENESS: competitors cannot easily imitate the distinctive advantage.

AVAILABILITY: consumers are willing to pay for the distinctive advantage.

PROFITABILITY: company can make a profit by marketing products with distinctive advantage.

CONFORMITY: the nature of distinctive advantage must be consistent with the current or the desired image of the company.[61]

As you can see, all these characteristics should be respected in order for the company to be able to fully benefit from the differentiation of its products in the market. In an ideal world, each company wants to achieve its competitive advantage at the lowest price, but achieving top quality at the same time. However, this is almost impossible to achieve in the real world. The current situation with suppliers in the market, now more than ever, is been using the following combinations of the positioning, such as "low price – acceptable quality level", "comfort- safety, design – resistance, product quality – post-sales service quality".[62]

As shown in practice, suppliers tend to highlight several competitive advantages at the same time, which carries in itself higher risks (unclear position in the market, overestimated/underestimated brand etc.). Since the positioning process may take years, even the smallest mistake may cost the company a lot of money.

For this very reason, each company must continuously invest in a quantitative market analysis, and monitor the position in the market as perceived by individual consumers, as well as the main competitors. In this way, the company will be able to identify the potential threat to its position or the opportunity to strengthen its current position in the market.

This is not a simple process, and this is where many companies fail. Why? In order for the company to be able to identify its so-called "target market", it needs to measure the market potential. In other words, it needs to identify and measure the current demand and to assess the future demand. The companies usually leave this task to experts. Such assessments are also very expensive. In this section, we are going to analyse the calculation of the current demand using a simple example, designed for all the companies that don't have any possibility to hire a professional expert in this area, and for all the companies that wish to find out how to determine the overall market demand by themselves.

Example:

Suppose we own a company which sells music CDs. In order for us to be able to identify our target market in detail, we must certainly assess the overall demand for music CDs in the capital.

We will use the following formula:

$Q = n \times q \times p$

where:

Q – total sales
n – number of consumers in the market
q – the average amount purchased by the consumer in one year
p – the average price of the product in the market.

According to the formula, let us assume that we have 100,000 consumers who buy 6 CDs on average, at an average price of €80. In this case, our overall demand amounts to €48,000, 000. In order for you to be able to calculate this, you must have all the afore-mentioned data, which you can obtain from a quality market research analysis. [63]

There is another simple method called the "chain ratio method", which correlates the known and the assumed data. The easiest way in which to use this method is for a company to include the data collected for the entire population, and then to separately make an assessment of who might be their potential buyers (based on market segmentation according to age, sex, income, education etc.). However, in order for you to be able to perform a high-quality market segmentation, we must clarify the following semantic traps, such as money, income, and wealth.

"The value of my knowledge and your knowledge, as separate, individual values, is two, as a sum, they make four, but as a whole, they make 5!"

HAVE YOU HEARD THE SCIENTIFIC TERM "BUTTERFLY EFFECT"?

"Small cause, large effect" – back in 1963, M. E. Lorenz proved that not a single physical system exhibits periodic behaviour.

The discovery which is known in economics as the "butterfly effect" is attributed to him. In other words, Lorenz interprets the way in which the flap of a butterfly's wings in Brazil can cause a tornado in Texas. If we consider his hypothesis in a literal sense, we could say that it is unrealistic, since butterfly hunters would exterminate them. However, Lorenz used this metaphor to show through the theory of unpredictability the propensity of a system to have a hypersensitive reaction to the slightest change.

The practice of underestimating specific issues, as well as an excessive self-esteem of the managers, can lead to a large-scale crisis because the managers cannot see the big picture. For this very reason, you need to ask yourself the following question: "What is it that I can do to make it easier for my managers to recognise the warning signs which foretell the upcoming crisis?"[64]

BETWEEN ORDER AND CHAOS!

In accordance with scientific and professional evidence submitted by the profession, according to the experience of the practitioners, the company receives early warning signs that are sometimes visible for up to one or two years before a crisis occurs.[65] However, managers often ignore such warning signs and concentrate all their efforts on the company's resources, hoping for a better outcome in the future. The scientific term used here is the "selective perception syndrome".

Let us take a look at the following example which could have been avoided by a plenary establishment of the early warning system:

- A company "A" suffers a record drop in the sales of its products, as well as a decline in margins, a negative cash flow, and liquidity issues. All these alarming signals have been ignored, and the company's management is focusing its management policy on the company's resources. Since the company is facing problems with liquidity, it is forced to go into debt (through overdraft loan rates and not fulfilling its financial obligations towards suppliers). Consequently, the suppliers are late in delivering the goods, and some suppliers may stop the entire delivery. This may cause a decrease in the production output level, delay in delivery to end customers and, as a result of this, the payment is not performed on time, but it is late. There are demotivation and fear among the employees. Quality workers start looking for another job, leaving the company. The company plunges into financial and market crisis, and faces some or all of the following problems: loss of market share, loss of profitability, a decrease in efficiency (losses), insolvency and illiquidity, leading to over-indebtedness.

These very problems are indicators of an early warning of the upcoming company's crisis. You may be wondering if the described situation could have been foreseen.[66]

ANTICIPATORY CRISIS MANAGEMENT – WHAAT??

Most crises can be managed and recognised. At this point, we need to mention that it is not essential just to establish an early warning system, but it is equally important to establish a quality early warning system. In other words, the system itself reports a special type of information to management which is a sufficient indicator of a timely alchemy of the company in the future. However, if the quality of such information is asymmetric, the crisis is imminent. There are several different methods used in the anticipatory crisis management, but in practice, we can divide them into five different phases, such as the following:

THE DETECTION OF MINOR SIGNALS

When analysing a company's environment, a focus should be placed on the so-called "micro signals" in the environment at informational, organisational, communication and psychological level. As all which is visible to the naked eye has been detected and identified already, it is essential to act preventively.

THE COMPARISON OF STRATEGIC PLANNING HYPOTHESES AND SCENARIO RESULTS

All the companies make strategic plans, irrespective of whether these plans are short-term, medium-term or long-term ones. However, there are just a few companies that, when designing such a strategic document, perform a simulation of scenario results as well. In other words, if a company, for example, decides to manufacture a product "Z", it needs to make the scenario that will show what kind of product placement would affect the rest of the product portfolio, price policy, distribution, competitors, market, the company's "goodwill", and if the product "Z" sales should fail, such a scenario will show to what degree this is going to affect the distribution, marketing, financial and market aspect of the company.

THE IDENTIFICATION OF DEVIATION

When establishing an early warning system within the company, it is of vital importance to know how to identify and filtrate the so-called "unimportant" signals from the "important" ones. This may lead to another problem, which is the problem of a too strong or a too weak filtering. In other words, if you choose the wrong "minor" signals with respect to their significance, the risk of the company's wrong strategic action is imminent.

STRATEGIC PLANNING

After having determined the micro risks, compared the hypotheses with scenario results, and identified deviations, it is necessary to determine the company's field of action using strategic planning techniques. In other words, an estimate is to be made as to the level at which the company is to concentrate all of its efforts and the level at which it will pay moderate or the slightest attention, as well as to the profit ratio for each of the three options separately.

COMPUTER SIMULATIONS OF ALTERNATIVES

Before taking any actions, it would be wise to perform their computer-based simulation, in order to shed light on some of the company's fields of action which may be anticipated at the very beginning of writing and designing of the business policy.[67]

As you can see, a crisis initiates with micro causes which may have huge consequences. Regardless of the potential risk it entails, in most cases it is predictable, and it has an end. When the crisis ends, we will be left with an experience from which we will be able to draw lessons. However, it is difficult to survive as many crises as we need to go through in order for us to be able to gain the necessary experience.

Today, we have the advantage because we can learn through the anticipatory action in order for us not to experience the bitter taste of the consequences. In this case, it is not important to focus all the concentration onto exact facts, and it is probably even more important to engage the imagination. The imagination enables you to design various types of potential planning scenarios using the project management techniques. Let us recall the following words of M. Forbes:

"Whoever claims that businessmen are only interested in facts, not in imagination, has obviously never read a five-year projection".

CHAPTER 6

CRISIS MEDIA MANAGEMENT

Key topics covered by this chapter

✓ We have got a Crisis in the Media! Beeep!!!

✓ John Stuart Mill! Does it ring any bells to you?

✓ The Counterstory

✓ "Somebody's lying! Who is it?"

✓ The Negative Spin Issue

✓ The Toxic Benzene in Drinking Water?!

✓ Shrunk tights!

✓ Hot PR Tricks!

CRISIS MEDIA MANAGEMENT

"When a crisis occurs, your goal is not to win, but to lose with a minimal difference!"

William Essex once said: "In the business world there is a rule - have some good ideas, but don't be too smart!" In the mid-nineties, a Scottish insurance company came up with the following idea: to send pigeons in boxes to some financial journalists. The pigeons were safely packed in boxes, and the very idea was for their delivery and release to serve as an original way of presenting the corporation's new products.

However, the outcome was different from what they expected. A columnist asked himself : "what would have happened if the pigeons had been delivered the previous day, or if the journalists had not been there to accept them and release them?"[68] Since communication is a crucial and indispensable part of marketing, a significant part of crisis management concerns the very information management. There is no company, institution or organisation that has not faced a crisis. However, even today when the role of the media is indispensable, there are organisations that believe they can "cover up" or "embellish"[69] the crisis.

WE HAVE GOT A CRISIS IN THE MEDIA! BEEEP!!!

Not only is this not a moral, ethical or legitimate approach, but it is also a completely wrong approach that can make the company incur huge losses due to the obtained bad public reputation. Then, they often go in search of the culprits, and usually, the first and biggest ones are journalists.

However, the role of a journalist is to convey information to the public, regardless of whether such information is positive or negative. For this very reason, journalism has got a massive responsibility, though this does not mean that journalists are the "culprits" only because they conveyed information to the public. You need to have a crisis management strategy ready, and all your employees must be familiar with it.

When a crisis occurs, do not wait for someone else to expose the crisis and to publish such information in the media. In this chapter, we are not going to show some good and bad examples of crisis management, but we are going to focus our attention on how they are handled in practice. When a crisis occurs, the first thing you need to do is to contact the most influential journalist you know.

Do not try to spiff up the crisis that has occurred, because all the people the journalist will contact concerning your case will try to apply their own *spin*. What matters is that you present the facts (without embellishment) and that what you do present is not only your side of the story, but the complete story. By doing so, you will become the primary source of the facts on the crisis. Journalists don't like spokespersons or PR experts too much since they are aware of the fact that they openly work for the interest of the opposite side. You can never turn a bad situation into a good one and do not try to do that. The objective of crisis management is to reduce the negative effect of a bad situation.[70] At this point, I will use some quotes by Napoleon:

"If I loosened the reins on the press, I would remain in power less than four months", or "Leaving the press to oneself means the same as falling asleep in front of danger".

JOHN STUART MILL! DOES IT RING ANY BELLS TO YOU?

He died in 1873, and this year remained known because it was thought that he was the last man who knew everything that could be known in the world.

He was a famous British economist, political thinker and philosopher. Today, the very idea that there is someone who could know all the known facts is ridiculous.[71] Today, we live in the age of knowledge and its dissemination; the amount of information is doubling every few years; scientific data is not limited anymore, and scientists have been publishing their latest findings in approximately 400,000 scientific publications worldwide.

Our habits have changed and we are prone to rapid and dynamic changes; we are getting in contact with ever more people; our relationships are shorter than ever; we are provided with a wide range of various products most of which tend to be forgotten by next year. To this day, we have developed the ability to synthesise and collect information, as well as to store and disseminate it. In the past, only large organisations had such power.

Today, the power of information is accessible to the entire population. For this very reason, information management is of vital importance, particularly in situations of crisis. Why is this important? Our modern age, that we often call "information age", has never been named the "age of knowledge". Information can never be literally interpreted as knowledge. It must be processed, which means that we need to assess it, absorb it, understand it, take it in and retain it.[72]

THE COUNTERSTORY

In a crisis situation, it is very risky to try to sell
a counterstory to the media.

For example, your chemical plant pollutes the environment to a large extent, but your biological fuel research laboratory is currently working on the steam engine car production. As can be seen from the above example, there is always a bright side, as well. Therefore, do not integrate the publishing of your counterstory into your crisis management strategy.

The counterstory is equal to avoiding the truth. Your goal is not to make the public look the other way, but to reduce the negative effect of a bad situation. Take a look at the following causal situation: after the September 11 attack tragedy that befell the USA on September 11th, 2001, Jo Moore, who served as a British special adviser and press officer, presented6 the following proposal: "Now is a good time to bury bad news."[73]

Most of the media that reported this obscene idea published the names of the organisations that published themselves bad news after the 9/11 tragedy (such as negative operating results etc.). This example shows that there is no competition in crisis management.[74]

"SOMEBODY'S LYING! WHO IS IT?"[75]

When a crisis occurs, at times there is information you are not allowed to publish, and if someone managed to get such information, the entire "picture" would take on a completely different form. Moreover, you may have found yourself in a situation in which the media were not looking "in the right direction" and if they knew only "one thing", they would understand everything. However, if you believe that someone should let the information "leak", it is very clear to the journalists that these are "purposeful leaks of information". For this very reason, do not let the "information leak". In crisis situations, you can do this only and exclusively with the journalist whom you trust[76].

THE NEGATIVE *SPIN* ISSUE

In order for you to be able to understand the problem of a negative *spin,* as well as its impact on your company in the times of crisis, first of all, you need to understand the way in which the media operate. A negative *spin* is always to the advantage of the media since it provides the other side of the story.

It sheds new light on the whole situation. Besides, you must be aware of the fact that there are readers who are only interested in negative issues. On the other hand, if we consider the statistical indicators, we have to admit the following: negative issues get a higher readership than the positive ones, and they expand the audience. Now, when you know all these facts, be sure not to try to turn the negative *spin* into the positive one. This is impossible to do, and most companies make a mistake by repeatedly attempting to do the "Sisyphean task"[77].

When the crisis occurs, there will be companies, people, and organisations that are not going to be interested in your success. It is important that you remain focused and composed, and that you present new information and facts. Your goal is not to argue, identify the culprits or blame someone else[78].

THE TOXIC BENZENE IN DRINKING WATER?!

Although I could cite some other examples in this section, I will only mention the cases which are used as postulates in crisis management. In 1990, the Perrier company's management was faced with the tragic news that traces of benzene were found in their mineral water bottles.

The Perrier corporation immediately published this information in the media and withdrew and destroyed 40 million water bottles, which cost the company 20 million pounds. During this entire event, the Perrier corporation was informing the public of each step that was taken in this respect. Do you know what was the outcome achieved by the Perrier company? Today, we are still drinking the Perrier water. As shown in the case of Perrier, the crucial issue that your company may be faced with upon the occurrence of a crisis is that if you do not manage it efficiently, it will deepen.

SHRUNK TIGHTS!

There is a case study which is often cited as an example in marketing courses, such as the following: one day, a lingerie manufacturer received a letter from one of its customers. Namely, the customer was not satisfied with the product and she complained to the manufacturer that her thights shrank when she tried to put it to dry on the stove.

Unfortunately, the concerned company replied to the lady with a message the meaning of which was the following: "Of course they shrank, stupid." The repercussions of this act were devastating for the company. The sales in the region dropped significantly because all the offended friends of the offended consumer started purchasing the products of another brand name. Although this example is a really drastic and radical one, it is very vivid, and it draws our attention to the important fact: "Never underestimate consumers and the public!".

Therefore, at the end, we will present the seven basic rules[79] in crisis management, which are as follows:

1. BE THE FIRST ONE TO PRESENT YOUR SIDE OF THE STORY
2. TELL THE STORY TO YOURSELF
3. TELL THE COMPLETE STORY
4. CHECK THE FACTS
5. DO NOT HIDE NEW INFORMATION
6. IF THERE IS SOMETHING THAT YOU DO NOT KNOW, SAY SO
7. BE ALWAYS AVAILABLE.

HOT PR TRICKS!

Underrepresentation in the media, as well as insufficient recognition being given to the work of an association, are a common problem for the majority of associations, mostly due to their limited financial resources and their lack of opportunity to hire experts. For this reason, most associations reduce their communication with the media to holding press conferences, though journalists have plenty of them to attend anyway. In order for your message to correspond to both the internal and external public, first of all, you need to define the association's mission and vision.

Defining the strategic plan of the association, its goals (both the short-term, medium-term and long-term ones), as well as establishing a quality internal hierarchy within the association, has a significant impact on the overall image of the association in public.

DEFINE A STRATEGIC PLAN OF THE PROMOTION

Identify the person who will be responsible for coordinating the promotion of the association, but it is also very important for all the members of the association to follow the "Strategic Promotion Plan" in order for you to be able to achieve the maximum efficiency through synergic action. In your strategic promotion plan, you need to clearly define the answers to the following questions: "What is the aim the association wants to achieve through promotion?", "What is the audience you are addressing?", "What kind of message do you want to convey to the public?", "What is your budget?"

Although the design of such a plan is really comprehensive and detailed, it provides you with a quality tool for a targeted appearance in public. Since the field of market communication is regulated by law in most countries, it would be a good idea to consult an expert before publicising your advertising message. As you are well aware yourself, your problem is scarce financial resources, and it is of vital importance to have high-quality preparation before appearing in the media. In addition to TV advertising and press advertising, along with the Internet advertising, you need to focus your attention on designing specific market activities aimed at attracting the media and informing the public. This refers for the most part to organising special business workshops which are necessary for the operation of the association.

UPDATE YOUR INTERNET MARKETING

When selecting different communication tactics, it is also important to update the association's website on a regular basis, and to be oriented towards the *e-mail* marketing, that is, to send *e-newsletters* to shareholders. The *e-newsletter* is one of the most efficient and quickest ways to improve the information flow, which also requires low investment costs.

In order for you to be able to match your image to your mission and vision and to convey your message to your target public as easy and as accurately as possible, your association needs to invest in printed materials (such as brochures, flyers, promo kits, posters etc.). Although it is not simple to do all the afore-mentioned at all, particularly with scarce financial resources available, in every association, there are members who are very skillful at fundraising from local entrepreneurs or from local self-government.

It is extremely important for all the members of the association to find a common language so as to avoid giving the wrong impression in public of your association not having clearly defined views on key issues. The easiest way to achieve this is by designing promotion materials that will contain basic information which is easy to remember and to understand for both the internal and the external public. Achieving a quality promotion and recognition in the media represents a long journey with numerous steps to take, not to skip, with its effects being visible only at the end of a specific media campaign.

At this point, the evaluation of the achieved goals is performed. However, although the expected results might contain some deviations, do not worry because you can always improve the undesired results in the following promotional campaign.

Every journey, including the one of the media,
starts with the first step.

CHAPTER 7

MARKETING FOR SMART ALECKS!

Key topics covered by this chapter

✓ Let's play the Game Theory

✓ The Prisoner's Dilemma

✓ Have you heard of the "fried egg strategy"?!

✓ I'm a Neuromarketing Genius!

✓ Hypnotising Titles- is this possible?!

✓ How many balls can you fit into a bus?!

MARKETING FOR SMART ALECKS!

If you could anticipate the "moves" of your competitors, you would work with less risk, wouldn't you? If you could find the answers to your questions in advance in politics, economics, mathematics and various military strategies, you would be much wiser! And you would be even wiser if you knew that an absolutely and relatively legitimate tool has been invented which you can use to obtain answers to questions such as the following: "What are my competitors planning to do with respect to pricing policy?", "Which market do they wish to enter?", "Is an advertising war imminent?"

GAME THEORY

No, no, not at all. You are not going to find such answers on the Internet or in the media, or in the published statistical, analytical or financial statements. You don't need the so-called "whistleblowers", since all you need is GAME THEORY. When it comes to the strategy/strategies, recent authors, writers, experts and scientists usually quote and rephrase various Japanese proverbs. Therefore, I will also follow their example. There is a Japanese expression which is used very much in the business world, and that is "Kosoryoku".

Unfortunately, its denotative meaning cannot be translated, but "Kosoryoku" means something like "your or your company's vision". However, this expression goes beyond its essential and formal form, and includes words such as "concept" and "imagination". "Kosoryoku" is the ability to "see what is invisible to the eye and to create a shape from an amorphous mass[80]." In other words, this is exactly what you need in developing a strategy.

Traditional schools and faculties have taught us specific techniques and tactics in strategy development. Today, the situation is quite different. You need to keep an open mind and avoid implementing traditional models at an early stage of the strategy development. You need to have a clear deviation in your mental process from the one of the others because this is the only way for you to be able to understand and learn how to implement Game Theory.

In 1944, John von Neumann and Oskar Morgenstern, (an eminent mathematician and economist, respectively, and both Nobel prize winners), jointly published a book which has linked Game Theory to economics for the first time, and which represents the beginning of search for a dynamic theory of interrelated theoretical decisions. Its application does not extend itself in terms of terminology or the conventional meaning of a "game", but it is used in analysing and resolving conflict situations, where the "players" have conflicting interests. For this reason, Game Theory is becoming an ever more important area of interest of the business society, and is being implemented in economics, politics, biology, sociology, psychology, linguistics, computer science etc.

Its official definition is the following: "It is a scientific discipline that studies the agents' rational behavioural interdependence, that is, the ways in which strategic interactions between rational players generate results depending on the priorities and preferences of the players". I personally prefer using the definition by Thomas C. Schelling, which is as follows: "These are the games in which, though secrecy may play a strategic role, there is some essential need for the signalling of intentions and the meeting of minds (which think alike). Finally, they are games in which what one player can do to avert mutual damage affects what another player will do to avert it, so that it is not always an advantage to possess initiative, knowledge or freedom of choice". So, how can this be applied in practice?

I will try to simplify this useful tool for you by breaking it down to basic principles in order for you to be able to implement it yourself in your day-to-day business operations.

Let us consider the following: every decision we make causally affects the decision of the others.

We also need to be aware of the fact that market is not an amorphous mass, and that our activities causally affect the behaviour and decisions of certain companies and enterprises. Accordingly, we can say that every final outcome is the sum of our numerous individual decisions and their mutual interactions that represent a specific product. In other words, the process leading to the final "product" represents a very long and complicated road.

By this, I don't mean the conventional, industrial, legal or technological one. I believe that every situation in which you find yourself, whether you make a good or a bad situation assessment, will determine your further course of action.

Well, you know this already. You also know that each situation your competitor finds himself in, whether you make a good or a bad assessment of it, will determine your future course of action, as well as the one of your competitor. However, do you know that there is a tool with the help of which you can anticipate your competitors' moves, as well as identify your course of action, and the one of your consumers? First of all, we need to clarify the basic Game Theory terminology.[81]

LET'S LEARN THE FUNDAMENTALS OF GAME THEORY!

"**Game**" – the term represents a description of strategic interactions the players can create. The "Game" is a set of rules describing the formal structure of a specific conflict situation.

"**Players**" – they are, for example, your business opponents/ competitors who devise strategies leading to different outcomes.

Game solution – a description of potential outcomes.

The Game's integrity – it includes all the moves aimed at a specific point leading towards an outcome.

Game Theory – it proposes reasonable solutions for specific groups of players and it studies their characteristics.

Like any game, this one has also got its limitations. However, it is impossible to handle all the information about your competitors. Consequently, it is impossible to anticipate all the potential "actions" of your "players". Therefore, it is not surprising that the behavioural economics has discovered that most people's decisions are based on the rational utility. For this reason, the evolutionary Game Theory also includes the biological and cultural element of its "players", as well as individual learning.[82]

THE PRISONER'S DILEMMA

The most common example of Game Theory is the so-called "Prisoner's dilemma". There are two suspects in a specific crime: Ian (I) and Mark (M), and the police put them in separate cells. Each suspect has two options: to admit or not to admit to the crime. If both suspects admit to the crime, they will be sentenced to five years in prison each. If one of them confesses, he will walk away free and testify against the other one who will face 20 years in prison. If none of them confesses, both of them will face one year in prison for misdemeanour. We can illustrate this game using the accompanying table. The analysis shows the following: from the analytical and mathematical perspective, it would be in the best interest of both of them not to admit to the crime. However, Ian's reasoning is the following: "If I don't admit to the crime, and Mark admits to it, I will serve 20 years instead of just one year. If I decide to admit to it, I might get away completely, or, if Mark confesses, I will face only 5 years in prison". However, Mark's reasoning is similar, so we can conclude that both of them are going to admit to the crime.

MARK

IAN	DOES NOT CONFESS	CONFESSES
DOES NOT CONFESS	1,1	20,0

Further analysis is to determine what would be better for Ian. Let us imagine that Ian will not even take into consideration the "confession" strategy. Thus, we have reduced it to the game shown in the accompanying table. However, now Mark's decision is simple: it is in his own best interest to confess. Thus, we have come to a unique strategy that both players will implement, which is the following: they will both confess. We could have started the procedure with Mark, as well. We can also repeat the same procedure as long as one of the players has a dominant strategy. The resulting reduced game will be the same, regardless of the order of execution of each elimination (except when two different strategies are the same for a specific player). The afore-mentioned procedure is called "the elimination of dominated strategies" and it represents the first step in solving numerous matrix games.[83]

MARK

IAN	DOES NOT CONFESS	CONFESSES
CONFESSES	0,20	5,5

What does this example show? This example shows how difficult it is to achieve mutual cooperation. Numerous businesses fail to achieve mutual cooperation, although it may have put them into a better position in the market. The logics of this so-called "Prisoner's dilemma"[84] is applied in many business situations (such as entering the market, expansion of business, hostile takeovers, supply chains, the adoption of standards, R&D, patents etc.) in which Game Theory provides various types of strategies that can be implemented. However, the most important thing that we can learn from this game is the following: usually, the organisational strategic management is not sequential or simultaneous as it is in the "game", but it contains an unknown mixture of both cases, with unknown "players" and a high degree of uncertainty. Since the potential actions between your competitors (players) are based on exclusive assumptions, Game Theory is a good strategy that will enable you to master your ability to change the course of your business. This is particularly important because, according to the latest studies, as much as 70 % of organisations that participated in the analysis have not made any improvements in terms of strategy in their business operation, while some organisations have even made their business go from bad to worse (research by Bain & Company)! I can conclude that most successful strategies are achieved by means of "complex systems of thought" by implementing the approach that seeks to integrate all the complex dependencies between actions and reactions of the players, aiming to do so in advance.

This is the reason why Game Theory will certainly find its place in your company, as well.

THE "FRIED EGG" STRATEGY

We often get flooded with ads promoting "added value" through purchase of a specific product. Why is this so? Let's take an egg, for instance. I can't help but ask you "Which came first, the chicken or the egg?" The egg, of course! Now, let's take a look at an egg. The consumer wants the whole egg! This means that the consumer wants both the yolk and the white. In other words, your consumer wants added value!

For this reason, you need to differentiate your service. You can do this in the following way: envelop your "egg yolk" (product) in the "egg white" in order to stand out from your competition and differentiate yourself in the market, and, of course, to become recognisable like the "fried egg" strategy.

Figure 2: Egg yolk and egg white

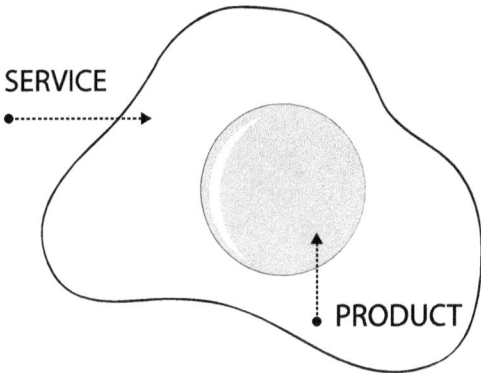

Source: Author.

In addition to products, efficient sales personnel and high-quality delivery, added value is always a source of competitive advantage that produces greater long-term effects than a one-time reduction in products' price. Moreover, competitive advantage is vital in building loyalty and close partnership relations with customers.

I'M A NEUROMARKETING GENIUS!

According to research data, one product in ten among the ones produced in the USA will fail. More specifically speaking, in 2005, more than 150,000 of new products failed, which, mathematically, means that the equivalent of the survival of new products in the market can be quantified in minutes. The Group XP Experience Index report (one of the largest research studies in the world which reports on the launching of new brands on the market),[85] among 21,000 new brands that were launched on the market last year, the 52 % of all the new brands and 75 % of individual products – FAILED!

If you remember the big research of Pepsi vs. Coca Cola, in which all the participants stated that Pepsi tasted better than

Coca Cola, Coca Cola surprisingly remained market leader and defeated Pepsi! Then dr. Montague, R. (2003), director of the Laboratory of Neuroscience at Baylor College of Medicine in Houston, (28 years after the testing was completed), decided to observe the entire case again in detail. At that time, he made a major discovery that has changed the entire view of the case.

The respondents who had drunk just a sip of Pepsi observed that it tasted much better than Coca Cola, though Coca Cola kept winning regardless of its taste. Then it was proved that emotions significantly affect our brain (when making a purchase decision or opting for a specific product) and that emotions have an effect on the value (the worth of it). Since Coca Cola has been evoking positive emotions in respondents throughout its history through its logotype, colours, design and smell, and has brought to the respondents' minds associations to their childhood, T-shirts with the Coca Cola logotype, shirts, prints on products etc., Coca Cola has achieved victory over the rational part of the human brain compared to Pepsi, regardless of its taste!

For this reason, neuromarketing has gone a step further from the subliminal communication and has included the whole interdisciplinary mix that triggers our emotions.

Since one book would not be enough to elaborate on this issue in detail, I have selected the part that you will be able to apply in practice, which refers to hypnotic titles and hypnotic words that evoke the effect of emotional appeal in us.

HYPNOTISING TITLES – IS THIS POSSIBLE?!

This chapter is not reserved only for marketing experts (marketers), but also for journalists who know very well that titles are the ones that sell a text/article/show etc.

We all know that it is very difficult to write an eye-catching title which no one will be able to resist and which will encourage readers to read the text. I had the same problem myself when I was coming up with the title for my book. However, if you are reading this chapter, I am glad that I have managed to get you interested in reading these pages. And now, let's get to work! Since technique, technique, and technique again is crucial in everything you do, thus we can say that good titles hide a scientific technique which has proven that there are specific titles that have the so-called "hypnotic effect" on the readers. How is this achieved? It is important that your title, irrespective of whether it is the title of a book, article, product name, newspaper story or similar, looks like a testimonial, not at all like an advertisement. Today you must have read some text in the newspapers (you were attracted by the title), and then you realised it was an advertisement. However, it is important that you have read it! This is – the key![86]

Our title should attract readers and keep them interested, and we are going to achieve this by using carefully selected words and/or expressions, which are as follows:

Find out
Learn
Discover
Save
Earn
Exclusive

Special report
How to...
Secret.[87]

Except for nouns, the title can include a combination of numbers and adjectives, such as the following:

The 2 best ways to
The 3 most powerful techniques
The 4 biggest secrets

I you wish to use emotional appeals, use the following words:

Exclusive
Fantastic
Fascinating
Phenomenal
Guaranteed
Unique
Finally
Announcement
Incredible
The first
Revolutionary
Powerful
Special
Improved
Successful
Exciting
Astonishing.[88]

HOW MANY BALLS CAN YOU FIT INTO A BUS?

Google is one of the best, the most desirable and the most respected employers ever! Everyone would like to work at Google, and only a few get such an opportunity! Why is this so? Today, it does not suffice for an applicant to claim that he or she is "super educated", a "super expert" etc., – one needs to have ... Whaaaat? Such questions are common for the companies looking for "that something"!

In 2009, Google advertised job vacancy in Croatia. Numerous candidates applied for the job because working conditions were excellent and the salary was extremely high in comparison to the average salary in Croatia. The candidates who were short-listed for the job had to answer 10 questions correctly, but these questions are not at all what you might expect! You can also try answering the 10 following questions and find out what are your chances to get a job at Google. A talented student of the Faculty of Electrical Engineering and Computing of the University of Zagreb has answered successfully all the 10 Google's job interview questions.

Let's start![89]

Why are manhole covers round?

You are shrunk to the height of a coin and your mass is reduced proportionally. You are thrown into a blender, the blades of which will start moving in 60 seconds. What will you do?

How much should you charge to wash all the windows in Seattle?

In three sentences, explain the word "database" to an eight-year-old.

There is a country in which the inhabitants only want boys, and every family continues to have children until they have a boy. If they have a girl, they have another child. If they have boy, they stop. What is the proportion of boys to girls in the country?

If the clock strikes 3.15, what is the angle between the hour and the minute hands? (The answer to this is not zero!)

How many pianos are there in the entire world?

Four people must cross a rickety rope bridge. Only one person has a torch, which, unfortunately, only has enough light left for seventeen minutes. The bridge is too dangerous to cross without a torch, and it is only strong enough to support two people at the same time, and each of them walks at a different speed. One can cross the bridge in one minute, another in two minutes, the third one in five minutes and the last one in ten minutes. How will they make it across all together in 17 minutes?

How many golf balls can fit into a school bus?

You are the captain of a pirate ship and your crew gets to vote on how you are going to split your gold. If fewer than half of the pirates agree with your proposal, you die. How would you recommend splitting the gold in a way that you get a good share of gold but still survive?

Would you like to know the answers? Read on.

Why are manhole covers round?

In Croatia, manhole covers are square. Round manhole covers are more easily moved when taken out.

You are shrunk to the height of a coin and your mass is reduced proportionally. You are thrown into a blender, the blades of which will start moving in 60 seconds. What will you do?

I will get onto the propeller hoping that the air flow would throw me out of the blender since I am very light.

How much should you charge to wash all the windows in Seattle?

Suppose that the hourly rate is $30. It takes 2 minutes for me to wash one window. This amounts to $1 per window. Seattle has half million inhabitants. Suppose there are 5 windows per capita (on a house, a business facility…). This amounts to $2.5 million. When we add life insurance, pension insurance, social security, other taxes, etc., this is $3 million in total.

In three sentences, explain the word "database" to an eight-year-old.

You and your classmates get grades in some subjects which are entered into the grade book. If she wishes to check your grades in a specific subject, the teacher knows exactly where to look. This is how a database works.

There is a country in which the inhabitants only want boys, and every family continues to have children until they have a boy. If they have a girl, they have another child. If they have boy, they stop. What is the proportion of boys to girls in the country?

If the probability of the birth of a boy and a girl is the same, the expected total number of boys and girls is the same.

If the clock strikes 3.15, what is the angle between the hour and the minute hands? (The answer to this is not zero!)

An angle of 7.5 degrees.

How many pianos are there in the entire world?

Suppose there is one piano per 1,000 inhabitants in each developed country. Let's assume there is a billion and half people living in developed countries. This means that there is a million and half pianos in the world in total.

Four people must cross a rickety rope bridge. Only one person has a torch, which, unfortunately, only has enough light left for seventeen minutes. The bridge is too dangerous to cross without a torch, and it is only strong enough to support two people at the same time, and each of them walks at a different speed. One can cross the bridge in one minute, another in two minutes, the third one in five minutes and the last one in ten minutes. How will they make it across all together in 17 minutes?

The first one and the second one will go first. It will take them 2 minutes. The first one will then come back. It will take him 1 minute. Then the third and the fourth one will cross the bridge. It will take them 10 minutes to cross it. The second one will then come back. It will take him 2 minutes. Finally, the first one and the second one will cross the bridge together. It will take them 2 minutes.

2 + 1 + 10 + 2 + 2 = 17 minutes

How many golf balls can fit into a school bus?

A school bus is about 15 metres long, 3 metres wide and 3 metres high. This is 135 cubic metres in total. We will approximate the golf ball as a cube with each side measuring 3 cm.

This amounts to 27 cubic centimetres. With a little calculation we get a total of 5 million golf balls in a bus.

You are the captain of a pirate ship and your crew gets to vote on how you are going to split your gold. If fewer than half of the pirates agree with your proposal, you die. How would you recommend splitting the gold in a way that you get a good share of gold but still survive?

I will split the gold into approximately equal amounts, and I will let them come to me in a specific order, letting each one take one part of it. I will take the remaining amount. If I split it into equal amounts, I will get the amount which is big enough.

Although these questions are part of the standard procedure for getting a job at Google, this is also an example of a high-quality marketing. Why? Using such questions, Google has obtained free space in different media.

CHAPTER 8

LET'S PLAY WITH YOUR MIND!

Key topics covered by this chapter

✓ The Out-of-the-box game

✓ A small creative Brain Teaser

✓ The Dot-To-Dot Game

LET'S PLAY WITH YOUR MIND!
THE OUT-OF-THE-BOX GAME

This game shows the way in which paradigms affect our perception of the environment and guide our reactions.

DESCRIBE WHAT YOU SEE IN THE PICTURE BELOW

Figure 3: What is in the picture?

Source: [90]

Did you see a funnel? Or two connected heads? A beautiful vase? A man and a woman? Two persons looking at one another?

There are countless answers to these questions and there is no wrong or correct answer. This figure can teach us that things are never what they seem. It's true, we have learnt all this when we were children. We were taught the following: "Don't believe what you see?!", or "Don't take candies from strangers, although they may look nice. You can only take candies from your mum, dad, grandma, grandpa etc."

Over the years, we have forgotten all this because life imposes its own rules and provides new perspectives. However, now is the right time to stop and take one, two, even five steps back, if necessary, to stop and to take a good look at the picture. The picture may regard our current "insurmountable" obstacle in business.

When we take a look at it for the first time, it will look dangerous and scary. If we take a look at it for the second time, we may see a funnel, and when we observe it for the third time, we might even see a beautiful vase! ☺

A SMALL CREATIVE BRAIN TEASER

Now, Let's boldly move on to another game! Draw a square with three lines not using the existing lines. See the illustration below.

Figure 4: Brain teaser

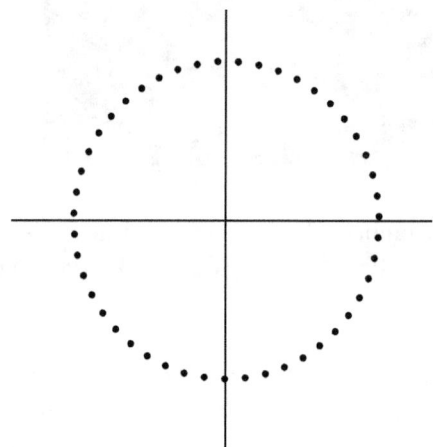

Source: [91]

Did you manage to do it??☺
GAME SOLUTION
Now, you should have obtained a drawing as shown in the following illustration:

Figure 5: Game solution

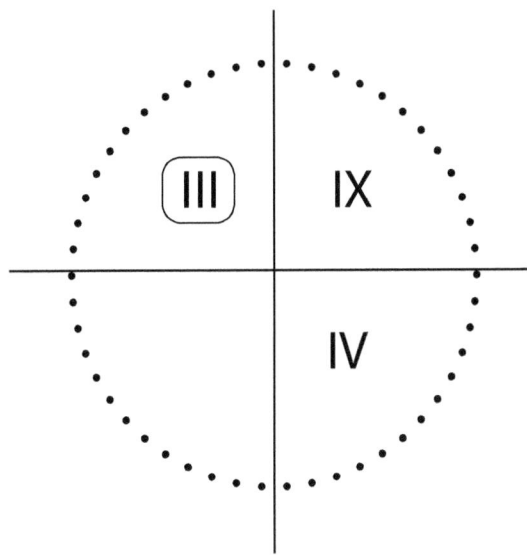

Source: [92]

This game has shown that the solution is always in the most simple things, or, let me rephrase what Einstein said:

"Imagination is more important than knowledge!"

To all of us who are in marketing, creativity is very important, as well as thinking "out of the box". Therefore, I truly hope that these tests will programme the grey matter in your brain to start functioning better and faster. Every time you are left with no inspiration, remember how important it is to play.

And finally, I have saved the most important text for last, which is as follows:

THE DOT-TO-DOT GAME

LEARN HOW TO EXTEND YOUR MIND AND YOUR FRAME OF REFERENCE!

Now, try to do something different. Connect all the dots with only four continuous strokes!

Figure 6: The dot-to-dot game

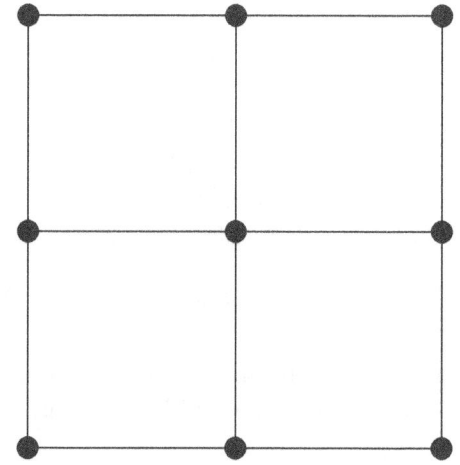

Source: [93]

It is imperative to LEARN FASTER THAN COMPETITORS! According to research conducted by the American Stanford University, the entire human knowledge originated by the year 1900, has already doubled in 1950. According to the same research, HUMAN KNOWLEDGE in the modern world of scientific and technological revolution gets doubled every 5-8 years. Therefore, the total number of innovations, patents, monographs, articles and other written products of the human mind is increasing in quantity at an incredible speed along the exponential curve, with the doubling time getting shorter. The premise is the following: the duration of the current situation and its projection in the future is not enough anymore. Prediction must rely on the following: a realistic identification of occurrences and events, as well as the identification of future needs.

The solution is shown below. If you have managed to do it, your drawing should look like this:

Figure 7: Game solution

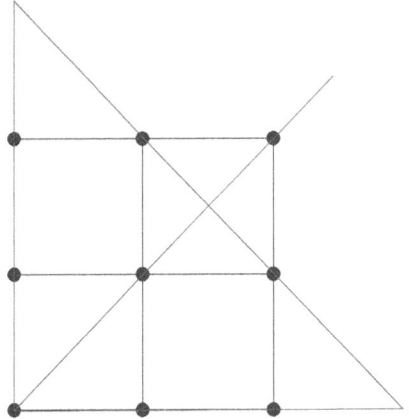

Source: [94]

BIBLIOGRAPHY

BOOKS
1. Bernays, E. 1952. *Odnosi s javnošću.* University of Oklahoma: Press.
2. Bull, G., 1961. *Translation of the Prince by Niccolo Machiavelli.* London: Penguin Books.
3. Bačun, D., 2009. *Priručnik o znakovima na proizvodima i ambalaži.* HR PSOR: Zagreb.
4. Cialdini, R.B.2007. *Utjecaj – znanost i praksa.* Mate: Zagreb.
5. Dicher, E., 1996.,*How Word of Mouth Advertising Works.*: E-knjiga: Harvard Business Review.
6. Essex,W., 2006. *Mogu li Vas citirati.* Papernet Limited: Velika Britanija.
7. Kotler Ph. i dr., 2006. *Osnove marketinga.* Mate: Zagreb.
8. Kržić, M. 2010. *Tehnike podsvjesne komunikacije.* E-knjiga:NewEra.
9. Lindstrom, M., 2009. Buyology: *How Everything We Believe about Why We Buy is Wrong.* Random House Business Books: London.
10. Mcluhan, M.,1962., *The Gutenberg Galaxy.* Routledge & Kegan Paul. E-knjiga: London.
11. Mucha, T., 2005. *This is your brain on advertising.* Business 2.0,35.
12. Mucha, T., 2005. *Why the caveman loves the pitchman.* Business 2.0.,35.
13. Ohmae, K., 2007. *Noval Globalna pozornica.* Mate d.o.o.: Zagreb.
14. Paliaga, M. 2007. *Branding i konkurentnost gradova*: Rovinj.
15. Porter, M. E. & Kramer., 2006., *M.R. Strategy and Society – The Link Between Competentive Advantage nad Corporate Social Responsibility.* E-knjiga: Harward Business Review.
16. Ruskoff, D., 1994. *Media Virus! Hidden Agendas in Popular Culture.* Ballantine Books: New York.

17. Reynolds, J. 2006. *Measurement and Analysis for Marketing.* Journal of Targeting, Vol. 14 No.3, pp.189-90.
18. Schiffman, L. G. i Kanuk, L. L., 2004. *Ponašanje potrošača sedmo izdanje.* Mate d.o.o. : Zagreb.
19. Waddock,S., 2004. *Parallel Universes-Companies.* Academics and the Progress of Corporate Citizenship Business and Society Review.
20. Vranešić, T.,Vignali C., Demetris V., 2004. *Upravljanje strateškim marketingom.* Accent: Zagreb.

RESEARCH PAPERS
1. Arndt, J., 1967. *Perceived Risk Sociometric Integration and Word of Mouth in the Adoption of a New Food Product.* Disertacija. Harvard University: Boston.
2. Bayus, B. L., 1984. *Word of Mouth and the Marketing Strategy A Model Integrating the Effects of Marketing Efforts and*
3. *Personal Influences for One Time Major Purchases.* Disertacija: University of Pennsylvania.
4. Day, S. G., 1971. *Attitude Change and the Relative Influence of Media and Word-Of-Mouth Sources:* Journal of Advertising Research.
5. Haramija, P., 2007. *Marketing usmenom predajom - fenomen mogućnosti.*Pregledni članak: UDK 658.8:659.144+659.186:2-425:17.036.2.
6. Omazić, M. A., 2007. *Društvena odgovornost i strategija hrvatskih poduzeća.* Doktorska disertacija. Sveučilište u Zagrebu, Ekonomski fakultet: Zagreb.
7. Piskóti, I., 2006. *Manuscript: Measurement of marketing campaigns.* University of Miskolc. Faculty of Economics: Marketing Institute.
8. Sudarević T., 2011. *Viralni marketing u sklopu Web 2.0. marketing strategije.* Ekonomski fakultet: Subotica.
9. Šola, H. M., 2013. *Neuromarketing - science and practice.* FIP – Scientific Journal of Effectus College for Law and

Finance with international peer-review: Volume 1, ISSN 1849-241 X.

10. Veljković, D. i Petrović, D., 2010. *Korporativna društvena odgovornost i značaj njezine promocije.* Pregledni rad: UDK 658:316.66.

INTERNET ARTICLES

1. Haumer, H., 2013. *Management zwischen Ordnung und Chaos u: Chaos Management.* The content is available on: <https://www.bilanz.de/management/ordnung>. [Retrieved on May 1st, 2016].

2. Chris Graves, 2014. *Ogilvy Worldwide PR.* The content is available on: <http://www.ogilvy.com/About/Ogilvy-and-Mather-Board/Chris-Graves.aspx.>. [Retrieved on May 1st, 2016].

3. *Greenwashing Report.*, 2010. The content is available on: <http://sinsofgreenwashing.com/findings/greenwashing-report-2010/. > [Retrieved on May 7th, 2016].

4. *Poslovni dnevnik. 2012. Čak 60% tvrtki u Hrvatskoj nema svoju web stranicu.* The content is available on: <http://www.poslovni.hr/marketing-i-mediji/cak-60-tvrtki-u-hrvatskoj-jos-nema-svoju-web-stranicu-203855>. [Retrieved on May 9th, 2016].

5. Stepper, J., 2013. *The Five Monkeys Experiment with a new lesson.* [Online] 26. October 2013. The content is available on:< http://goo.gl/XnhN8N>. [Retrieved on May 12th, 2016].

6. Škare, V. 14. 06. 2010 *asistent na Ekonomskom fakultetu u Zagrebu,* intervju., autor: Ivan Jozić, Marketing i prodaja.

7. Teklić.hr., 2014. *Nakon 9 godina 22% stranice the Milion Dollar Homepage je mrtvo.* The content is available on: http://www.teklic.hr/tag/the-million-dollar-homepage/. [Retrieved on May 9th, 2016].

PROFESSIONAL ARTICLES
1. Vlastelić, A., Stolac, D., Stolac, D., 2015. *Idemo se igrati. Reklame za djecu predškolske dobi.* Odjel za kroatistiku. Filozofski fakultet: Sveučilište u Rijeci.

LECTURE HANDOUTS
1. Paliaga, M., Mihovilović, J. 2014. *Marketing putem društvenih mreža.* Predavanja: Sveučilište u Rijeci, Katedra za marketing.
2. Šola, H. M., acad. year 2013/2014, *lectures at the Kairos College for Public Relations and Media Studies,* course title: Public Relations in the Non-profit sector. Lecturer: Šola, H. M.

SCIENTIFIC JOURNALS
1. Bird, R. et.al., 2007. *What Corporate Social Responsibility Activities are Valued by Market?.* Journal of Business Ethics.
2. Davenport, T.H., 1997. *Information Ecology.* Oxford University Press.
3. Društvo za zaštitu potrošača. 2010., *RealEyes Sustainability:* UK.
4. Fugate, D., 2009. *Marketing services more effectively with neuromarketing research: a look into the future.* Journal of Services Marketing .Vol.22 Issue 2: London.
5. Fugate, D., 2007. *Neuromarketing: a layman's look at neuroscience and its potential application to marketing practice.* Jorunal of Consumer Marketing Vol. 24 issue 7:London.
6. Global Media Deck., 2010. *Image Power Green Brands Survey.*
7. Mucha, T., 2005. *This is your brain on advertising.* Business 2.0, 35. (August): NJ.
8. Mucha, T., 2005. *Why the caveman loves the pitchman.* Business 2.0, 6(3): NJ.
9. Perrachione, T. Perrachione, J., 2008. Brains and Brands: *Developing mutually informative research in neuroscience and marketing.* Jorunal of Consumer Behaviour. Vol. 8 issue 5: London.

- Reynolds, J., 2006. *Measurement and Analysis for Marketing.* Journal of Targeting Vol. 14 No.3: London.
- Ribar, M.,2002.,*Proturječno usmeno reklamiranje:* Privredni vjesnik, br. 3269.
- Schor., J. B. 2004. *Born to Buy. Ch.9. The Debate about advertising and marketing to kids.* Advertising Educational Foundation.
- Šola, H.M., 2013. *Neuromarketing - science and practice.* FIP – Scientific Journal of Effectus College for Law and Finance with international peer-review: Volume 1, ISSN 1849-241 X.

JOURNAL ARTICLES
1. Šola, H. M., 2013. *Medijsko upravljanje kriznim situacijama.* Poslovni Savjetnik.. ISSN 1845-092X Br.99.: Zagreb
2. Šola,H. M., 2013. *NeuroPR-Što mogu OJ naučiti iz Neuromarketinga.* Poslovni Savjetnik. ISSN 1845-092X Br.98.: Zagreb
3. Šola, H. M., 2013. *Primjena marketinga uz dozvolu.* Poslovni Savjetnik. ISSN 1845-092X Br.97.: Zagreb
4. Šola, H. M., 2013. *Teorija igara-važan alat za razvoj strategije.* Poslovni Savjetnik. ISSN 1845-092X Br.96.: Zagreb
5. Šola, H.M., 2013. *Pozicioniranje tvrtke u recesijskim uvjetima.* Poslovni Savjetnik. ISSN 1845-092X Br.93.: Zagreb
6. Šola, H. M., 2012. *Greenwashing ili zeleno pranje.* Poslovni Savjetnik. ISSN 1845-092X Br.92.: Zagreb
7. Šola, H. M., 2012. *Dječji marketing – Igroglasi.* Poslovni Savjetnik. ISSN 1845-092X Br.89.: Zagreb.
8. Šola, H. M., 2012. *Efekt leptira u managementu tvrtke.* Poslovni Savjetnik. ISSN 1845-092X Br.86.: Zagreb
9. Šola, H. M., 2012. *Prikriveni ekonomski pokazatelji.* Poslovni Savjetnik. ISSN 1845-092X Br.84.: Zagreb

10. Šola, H. M., 2012. *Kompetitivna inteligencija u poslovanju.* Poslovni Savjetnik. ISSN 1845-092X Br.83.:Zagreb
11. Šola, H. M., 2012. *Neuromarketing-Znanost u službi kupca.* Poslovni Savjetnik. ISSN 1845-092X Br.82.:Zagreb
12. Williams G., 1989. *Comparative Media Study.* Princeton University Press 22.50: NJ.
13. Wannamaker, J., 1876. *Publicité Montréal Publicité Cognitive*: Montreal.

CONFERENCE PAPERS

1. Alčaković, S., 2011. *Neuromarketing-nov način razumevanja potrošača.* 8. Naučni skup sa međunarodnim učešćem Sinergija: Beograd.

ABOUT THE AUTHOR

Dr.Hedda Martina Šola has been listed in the International Encyclopaedia written by R. Hübner, entitled "Who is Who in Croatia"(2015) among the leading marketing experts in Croatia. She drew on her rich twenty-year professional experience in marketing at strategic positions within different companies as a Board Member for Marketing. Until recently, she held the position of Vice-Dean for business cooperation and international relations at the University College of Economics, Entrepreneurship and Management, and today she is a university professor teaching at several private faculties in the Republic of Croatia and advisor to leading companies in the market. She is also a regular guest at international conferences and congresses where she gladly gives lectures in two foreign languages. To this day, she has advised more than 100 different companies on how to develop their brands, strengthen their market position in terms of strategy, and to reposition themselves in the market. She has also published more than 30 scientific and professional papers on the topic of marketing and neuromarketing, peer-reviewed at both national and international level.

She worked for the Government of the Republic of Croatia (TIPA) where she was responsible for marketing development at the national level and is the author and co-author of several marketing projects supported by the Croatian Government, as well as of the marketing strategy of various towns and municipalities. She was educated in Croatia and the USA (Cleveland State University, FIAS- Washington DC, Cambridge Wealth Management), as well as at the University of Copenhagen, Copenhagen Business School, Denmark, at which she obtained her specialisation in neuromarketing and consumer neuroscience.

She is the author of the first book on neuromarketing published in Croatia under the title Marketinška oružarnica. She has won numerous awards and recognitions, and her passion for marketing and science has led her to the doctorate in Economic Science with specialisation in Neuromarketing.

She has obtained her Doctoral Degree in Neuromarketing at the Hercegovina University, Faculty of socio-economic Sciences. She is a registered marketing court expert at the County Court in Zagreb and a much quoted interlocutor in the media. For more information about the author, please visit the following web site: www.heddamartinasola.com.

ENDNOTES

1 op.cit.: Lindstrom, M., 2008. Buyology. Published in United States by Doubleday Publishing Group: New York.

2 The technical term "reward and reinforcement" was coined by dr. Henrik Walter, a psychiatrist and a neuroscientist who participated in the study together with marketing experts.

3 cfr: Stepper, J., 2013. The Five Monkeys Experiment with a new lesson. [Online] October 26th, 2013. The content is available on:< http://goo.gl/XnhN8N>. [Retrieved on May 12th, 2016].

4 op. cit.: Davenport, T.H., 1997. Information Ecology. Oxford University Press.

5 cfr.: Ackam. 1997.

6 op. cit.: Šola, H. M.,2012. Dječji marketing – Igroglasi., Poslovni Savjetnik. Br.89.:Zagreb.

7 Ibidem.

8 cfr.:Vlastelić, A., Stolac, D., Stolac, D., 2015. Idemo se igrati. Reklame za djecu predškolske dobi. Odjel za kroatistiku. Filozofski fakultet: Sveučilište u Rijeci.

9 Ibidem.

10 Ibidem.

11 op.cit.: Šola, H.M.,2012. Neuromarketing-Znanost u službi kupca., Poslovni Savjetnik. Br.82.: Zagreb.

12 cfr: the study was published in the scientific journal of Princeton University,(June 10, Issue of Science – 2005), supervised byA. Todorov,and N. Oosterhof,an assistant of the professor of psychology.

13 op.cit.: Perrachione, T. & Perrachione, J. (2008), Brains and Brands: Developing mutually informative research in neuroscience and marketing, Journal of Consumer Behaviour, Vol 8, issue 5, pp. 303-318.

14 op.cit.: Wannamaker J. (1876), Publicité Montréal Publicité Cognitive.

15 Ibidem.

16 op.cit.: Lindstrom, M., 2008. Buyology. Published in United States by Doubleday Publishing Group: New York.

17 cfr: Ibidem.

[18] Ibidem. Note: The research team was supervised by dr. Gemma Calvert, University of Warwick, England and prof. Richard Silberstein, CEO at Neuro-Insight in Australia.

[19] op.cit.: Šola, H.M., 2013. Neuromarketing - science and practice. FIP – Scientific Journal of Effectus College for Law and Finance with international peer-review: Volume 1, ISSN 1849-241 X.

[20] cfr.: Lindstrom, M.,2009. Buyology: How Everything We Believe about Why We Buy is Wrong. London: Random House Business Books.

[21] Šola, H.M., 2013. Neuromarketing - science and practice. FIP – Scientific Journal of Effectus College for Law and Finance with international peer-review: Volume 1, ISSN 1849-241 X.

[22] Ibidem.

[23] op.cit.: Alčaković S. (2011), Neuromarketing-nov način razumevanja potrošača, 8. Naučni skup sa međunarodnim učešćem, Beograd, p.277.

[24] Ibidem, 21.

[25] Ibidem.

[26] Ibidem.

[27] op.cit.: Bernays, E. 1952. Public Relations. University of Oklahoma: Press.

[28] op.cit.: Šola, H.M.,2013. NeuroPR-Što mogu OJ naučiti iz Neuromarketinga., Poslovni Savjetnik. Br.98.:Zagreb.

[29] op.cit.: Cialdini, R.B.2007. Utjecaj – znanost i praksa. Mate: Zagreb.

[30] op.cit. Chris Graves, Ogilvy Worldwide PR.

[31] op.cit.: Cialdini, R.B.2007. Utjecaj – znanost i praksa. Mate: Zagreb.

[32] cfr.: Ibidem.

[33] op.cit.: Šola, H.M.,2013. NeuroPR-Što mogu OJ naučiti iz Neuromarketinga., Poslovni Savjetnik. Br.98.:Zagreb.

[34] op. cit.: Šola, H. M., 2012. Kompetitivna inteligencija u poslovanju., Poslovni Savjetnik. Br.83.:Zagreb.

[35] Ibidem.

[36] op. cit.: Šola, H. M., 2013. Primjena marketinga uz dozvolu, Poslovni Savjetnik. Br.97.: Zagreb.

[37] Ibidem.

[38] cfr.: Godin, S., 2013. Seth Godin's Blog.

[39] op. cit.: Šola, H. M., 2012. Greenwashing ili zeleno pranje, Poslovni Savjetnik. Br.92.:Zagreb.

[40] cfr.: Greenwashing Report., 2010.

[41] op. cit.: Šola, H. M., 2012. Greenwashing ili zeleno pranje, Poslovni Savjetnik. Br.92.:Zagreb.

[42] op. cit. Bačun, D., 2009. Priručnik o znakovima na proizvodima i ambalaži. HR PSOR: Zagreb.

[43] Ibidem.

[44] Ibidem.

[45] cfr.: The Consumer Protection Association., RealEyes Sustainability., 2010. UK.

[46] cfr.: Global Media Deck, 2010. Image Power Green Brands Survey.

[47] op.cit. Retrieved on January 10th, 2017 from http://leanwashingindex.com/the-lowdown/naked-juices/

[48] op. cit.: Šola, H. M., 2013. Pozicioniranje tvrtke u recesijskim uvjetima. Poslovni Savjetnik. Br.93.:Zagreb.

[49] op.cit. Retrieved on January 10th, 2017 from http://www.lse.ac.uk/economics/aboutUs/nobelPrizeAwardedAlumni.aspx

[50] op. cit.: Šola, H. M., 2012. Prikriveni ekonomski pokazatelji, Poslovni Savjetnik. ISSN 1845-092X Br.84.:Zagreb.

[51] Ibidem.

[52] Ibidem.

[53] Ibidem.

[54] op. cit.: Cialdini, R. B. 2007. Utjecaj – znanost i praksa. Mate: Zagreb.

[55] Ibidem.

[56] Author's comment: the principle of perceptual contrast is not a technique used in psychology, but it refers to the way in which a specific request is structured. For example, if you wish to borrow € 100 from someone, and you start with € 50, there is no way you can lose. If you accept, you will get twice as much as you were willing to accept. If you don't, you will reduce the amount to € 50, and you will get what you were planning to get from the very beginning.

[57] op. cit.: Cialdini, R. B. 2007. Utjecaj – znanost i praksa. Mate: Zagreb.

[58] Ibidem.

[59] op. cit.: Šola, H. M.,2013. Pozicioniranje tvrtke u recesijskim uvjetima. Poslovni Savjetnik. ISSN 1845-092X Br.93.:Zagreb.

[60] op. cit.: Vranešić, T.,Vignali C., Demetris V., 2004. Upravljanje strateškim marketingom. Accent: Zagreb.

[61] Ibidem.

[62] Ibidem.

[63] op. cit.: Šola, H. M.,2013. Pozicioniranje tvrtke u recesijskim uvjetima. Poslovni Savjetnik. ISSN 1845-092X Br.93.:Zagreb.

[64] op. cit.: Šola, H. M.,2012. Efekt leptira u managementu tvrtke Poslovni Savjetnik. ISSN 1845-092X Br.86.:Zagreb.

[65] op. cit. Haumer, H., 2013. Management zwischen Ordnung und Chaos u: Chaos Management.

[66] op. cit.: Šola, H. M.,2012. Efekt leptira u managementu tvrtke Poslovni Savjetnik. ISSN 1845-092X Br.86.:Zagreb.

[67] Ibidem.

[68] op. cit.: Essex, W. 2006. Can I Quote You on That? Papernet Limited: Great Britain.

[69] op. cit.: Šola, H. M., 2013. Medijsko upravljanje kriznim situacijama Poslovni Savjetnik. ISSN 1845-092X Br.99.:Zagreb.

[70] op. cit.: Šola, H. M., 2013. Medijsko upravljanje kriznim situacijama Poslovni Savjetnik. ISSN 1845-092X Br.99.:Zagreb.

[71] Ibidem.

[72] op. cit.: Cialdini, R.B.2007. Utjecaj – znanost i praksa. Mate: Zagreb.

[73] Source: Wikipedia.

[74] op.cit.: Essex, W. 2006. Can I Quote You on That? Papernet Limited: Great Britain.

[75] On Dec. 29th, 2016 Hillary Clinton gave an interview to the Editorial Board of The Conway Daily Sun. The content is available on: http://www.steynonline.com/7404/somebody-lying-who-is-it. [Retrieved on Jan 18th, 2017].

[76] op.cit.: Essex, W. 2006. Can I Quote You on That? Papernet Limited: Great Britain.

[77] Author's Comment: a metaphor for useless work or pointless actions.

[78] op.cit.: Essex, W. 2006. Can I Quote You on That? Papernet Limited: Great Britain.

[79] Ibidem.

[80] op. cit.: Ohmae, K., 2007. Noval Globalna pozornica. Mate d.o.o.: Zagreb.

[81] op. cit.: Šola, H. M., 2013. Teorija igara-važan alat za razvoj strategije. Poslovni Savjetnik. ISSN 1845-092X Br.96.:Zagreb.

[82] Ibidem.

[83] op. cit. Retrieved from: decision.math.hr/nastava/vježbe/02-primjeri nashovog equilibriuma.pdf/. [Retrieved on May 12th, 2016].

[84] Ibidem.

[85] cfr: XP Marketing Group.

[86] op. cit.: Kržić, M. 2010. Tehnike podsvjesne komunikacije.E-knjiga:NewEra.

[87] Ibidem.

[88] Ibidem.

[89] op. cit.: Jutarnji list, autor: Arslani M., : Želite posao? Koliko lopti stane u bus?, [Published on Nov 9th, 2009].

[90] The figure was retrieved from the PPT presentation by Šola, H. M., acad. year 2013/2014, lectures at the Kairos College for Public Relations and Media Studies, course title: Public Relations in the Non-profit sector. Lecturer: Šola, H. M.

[91] Ibidem.

[92] Ibidem.

[93] Ibidem.

[94] Ibidem.

FIGURE

TABLE

AND PLEASE...

If you'd like more quality neuromarketing at
this low price, I'd really appreciate a review
accumulates on a daily basis has a direct
impact on how it sells, so just leaving a review,
no matter how short, helps make it possible for
me to continue to do what I do. Here's a link
to leave a review on Amazon:

http://bit.do/neuromarketing_armoury

www.ingramcontent.com/pod-product-compliance
Lightning Source LLC
Chambersburg PA
CBHW051706170526
45167CB00002B/551